THE
SCIENCE OF
NUTRITION

FOOD AND SOCIETY

THE SCIENCE OF NUTRITION

Edited by Kara Rogers, Senior Editor, Biomedical Sciences

Britannica®
Educational Publishing

IN ASSOCIATION WITH

ROSEN
EDUCATIONAL SERVICES

Published in 2013 by Britannica Educational Publishing
(a trademark of Encyclopædia Britannica, Inc.) in association with Rosen Educational Services, LLC
29 East 21st Street, New York, NY 10010.

Distributed exclusively by Rosen Educational Services.
For a listing of additional Britannica Educational Publishing titles, call toll free (800) 237-9932.

First Edition

Britannica Educational Publishing
J.E. Luebering: Senior Manager
Marilyn L. Barton: Senior Coordinator, Production Control
Steven Bosco: Director, Editorial Technologies
Lisa S. Braucher: Senior Producer and Data Editor
Yvette Charboneau: Senior Copy Editor
Kathy Nakamura: Manager, Media Acquisition
Kara Rogers, Senior Editor, Biomedical Sciences

Rosen Educational Services
Jeanne Nagle: Senior Editor
Nelson Sá: Art Director
Cindy Reiman: Photography Manager
Marty Levick: Photo Researcher
Brian Garvey: Designer, Cover Design
Introduction by Kara Rogers

Library of Congress Cataloging-in-Publication Data

The science of nutrition/edited by Kara Rogers.
    p. cm. — (Food and society)
"In association with Britannica Educational Publishing, Rosen Educational Services."
Includes bibliographical references and index.
ISBN 978-1-61530-920-7 (lib. bdg.)
1. Nutrition. I. Rogers, Kara.
QP141.S3484 2013
613.2—dc23

                                                              2012011482

Manufactured in the United States of America

CONTENTS

5

15

22

$$- CH = CH - \overset{\overset{\displaystyle CH_3}{|}}{C} = CH -$$

62

63

77

84

89

94

CH. 5: Nutritional Irregularities 93

CH. 6: Vitamin Deficiency and Toxicity

147

159

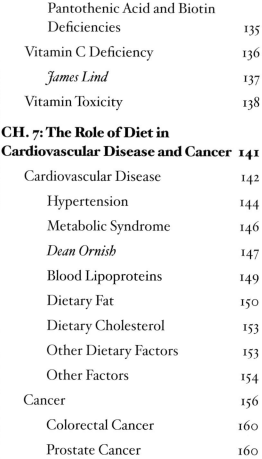

173

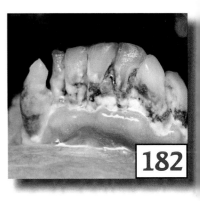

182

187

190

INTRODUCTION

Over the course of decades, scientists have conducted fascinating investigations into human nutrition, discovering, demonstrating, and confirming the fundamental role that food and nutrients fulfill in human life. As elucidated in this volume, among the many important functions of nutrients are enabling growth and development, preventing disease, and providing energy for activities ranging from chemical reactions in cells to the contraction of muscles during exercise. The science of nutrition, as it is explored in these pages, offers readers insight into the interactions between nutrients and tissues, the properties of the nutrients themselves, and the role of nutrition in health and disease.

The journey begins with an exploration of the relationship between food and the human body. Food is a source of energy that the body accesses through the processes of digestion and metabolism. These processes free from foods the nutrients needed to fuel chemical reactions and break down or build up materials such as tissues. The work of performing these activities is associated with the production of heat. This heat energy is measured in kilocalories or, put simply, calories. The number of calories in food is determined using an instrument known as a bomb calorimeter, which measures the amount of heat released when a food is burned completely.

A young woman enjoys a nutritious fruit salad. Reggie Casagrande/The Image Bank/Getty Images

The calorie is a key component of modern nutrition, appearing on the nutrition labels that grace a variety of foods and beverages, and being used as a general guideline for each individual's daily food requirements. For example, a 125-pound woman who is moderately active requires 2,000 calories each day to meet her energy needs, whereas a 175-pound male who is very active requires as many as 3,000 calories each day. Overconsumption or underconsumption of calories leads to weight gain or weight loss, respectively.

But nutrition is more than simply counting calories to maintain a balance between energy intake and energy expenditure. The type of food that calories come from, for instance, influences the efficiency with which cells and tissues carry out their functions. To assist people with planning a healthy diet that contains adequate quantities of nutrients from each of the basic food groups (e.g., fruits and vegetables, grains, meat, and milk and milk products), many governments worldwide have established dietary and nutrient recommendations. Scientific evaluation of nutritional requirements led to the development in 1941 by the U.S. National Academy of Sciences of Recommended Daily Allowances (RDAs), or the amount of each type of nutrient needed to maintain health. In the 1990s in the United States and Canada, RDAs were replaced with Daily Reference Intakes (DRIs), values that provide more comprehensive information than RDAs alone. For each essential nutrient, there are four DRI values: Estimated Average Requirement, Recommended Daily Allowance, Adequate Intake, and Tolerable Upper Intake Level. This categorization helps prevent individuals from consuming too much or too little of any one essential nutrient.

Essential nutrients are those that must be consumed in the diet because the body does not produce them or does not produce them in quantities sufficient for survival. The essential nutrients found in foods are divided into two major groups, the macronutrients and the micronutrients. Whereas macronutrients supply the bulk of nutrients, micronutrients are needed only in very small amounts. These two groups can be further subdivided into five classes: carbohydrates, lipids, and proteins (the macronutrients), and vitamins and minerals (the micronutrients). Water forms a sixth class of essential nutrient.

The body derives most of its energy from carbohydrates, which include starches and sugars. The most important of these is the sugar glucose, a tightly regulated source of energy for cells that serves as the primary fuel for the brain. Lipids, which include fats and oils, fulfill a variety of roles in the body, from maintaining cell membrane flexibility to being stored in the form of adipose tissue, which pads vital organs and acts as an energy reserve. Lipids also transport fat-soluble vitamins through the blood and are responsible for producing a sense of fullness, or satiety, following a meal. The major type of lipid is triglyceride, of which there are different forms, each being made up of chains of fatty acids. The proteins, the last of the macronutrients, are the structural molecules of the body and are abundant in muscle, bone, and skin, as well as in hair and nails.

Although vitamins are best known by their letter designations, A, C, D, E, K, and the B complex, some are referred to by their chemical names (e.g., biotin and folic acid). Based on their chemical properties, vitamins can be divided into two groups, water-soluble (C and the B complex), which dissolve in water and are readily excreted in urine, and fat-soluble (A, D, E, and K), which are absorbed by lipids and tend to accumulate in the body. All vitamins play important regulatory roles in metabolism. For instance, water-soluble vitamins catalyze the transfer of energy between molecules and the metabolism of macronutrients, while fat-soluble vitamins regulate the production of proteins and form structural and functional components of biological membranes.

Minerals are unique from all other essential nutrients in that they are not metabolized and often are present in the body in the form of salts, which are positively and negatively charged ions bound together. Among their primary functions are governing the flow of water across cell membranes, giving strength to bones, and serving as components of larger molecules. Calcium and phosphorus are the two most abundant minerals in the human body, owing to their high concentrations in bone. Other so-called macrominerals, for which daily requirements are 100 mg or more, include chloride, magnesium, potassium, sodium, and sulfur. Minerals required in smaller amounts, typically 15 mg or less, are known as microminerals, or more commonly, trace minerals. These include chromium, cobalt, copper, fluoride, iodide, iron, manganese, molybdenum, selenium, and zinc. Minerals required in microgram quantities, such as aluminum and boron, are known as ultratrace elements.

The essential nutrients are distributed across nine different food groups. Cereals, such as corn, rice, and wheat, form the most important food group for many societies worldwide, in part because they are easily grown, staving off hunger, and in part because they readily supply the body with the large amounts of carbohydrate it requires. Other sources of carbohydrates include starchy roots and legumes. The latter also serve as a source of protein, and both starchy roots and legumes are important sources of vitamins, as are fruits and vegetables. Fruits and vegetables also are high in water but low in protein and fat (although some fruits, such as dried coconut, olives, and particularly avocados, contain fat). In contrast, oils, butter, and lard are rich sources of fat. Meat and fish also contain relatively large amounts of fat and, along with eggs, are key sources of protein, minerals, and vitamins. Vitamins are also abundant in milk and milk products, which further serve as major sources of calcium.

The science of nutrition also explores the mechanisms that regulate the intake of food and the biological significance of nutritional irregularities, including deficiencies and toxicities. A lack of nutrients can trigger specific hungers, which may be satisfied by eating a certain type of food. In other cases, there is insufficient intake of calories, leading to the stimulation of the hunger centre, which is located in the lateral hypothalamus of the brain. When the hunger centre is activated, individuals feel a strong urge to eat. This true feeling of hunger is fundamentally different from the general desire to consume food, particularly certain types of foods, which is known as appetite. Appetite is determined by various chemicals in the body, including hormones and neurotransmitters, which may be activated by the smell or flavour of food and serve as a communication link between the gastrointestinal tract and the brain. Chemicals that suppress appetite and factors such as satiety are examples of mechanisms that limit food intake.

Nutritional irregularities underlie numerous diseases and disorders in humans and may arise from any of a number of causes, including a lack of access to food, under- or overconsumption, hereditary disorders, developmental abnormalities, and environmental factors such as food allergies, food-drug interactions, and the contamination of food with chemicals or infectious agents. The most prevalent nutritional disorder in the world, affecting some 925 million people, is chronic undernutrition, which often is associated with agricultural deficits or social issues such as poverty. Persistent undernutrition may eventually compromise physiological functions such as metabolism and thus is considered a form of malnutrition. Malnutrition can also be caused by overnutrition, by poor diet (i.e., eating foods of little nutritional value), and by diseases or disorders that block the absorption or metabolism of nutrients.

Even the most prosperous societies are not free from nutrition-related disease. Indeed, access to an abundance of food can come with costly health consequences, which typically manifest in the form of conditions such as obesity, cardiovascular disease, and diabetes. Moderation, then, is key. Another growing problem in all countries worldwide is the impact of poor diet on health and the resulting rise in chronic disease, particularly cardiovascular disease and diabetes. Multiple dietary factors, rather than the absence or presence of a single nutrient, are implicated in these conditions, and therefore the act of improving one's overall diet can have a significant impact on treating these diseases.

Vitamin and mineral deficiencies are among the best-studied nutritional disorders. Indeed, the discovery in the early 20th century of thiamin deficiency and vitamin C deficiency as the causes of beriberi and scurvy, respectively, opened the door to the discovery of other vitamins and vitamin-associated diseases. Likewise, the high incidence of anemia and the susceptibility to poor neuromuscular development and cretinism (short stature, intellectual disability, and developmental abnormalities) in some parts of the world led to the characterization of iron and iodine deficiencies. Many micronutrient deficiencies are readily prevented through supplementation or the fortification of foods. However, for individuals who already consume adequate amounts in their diets, additional quantities, especially when consumed in supplements, can lead to micronutrient toxicity, which may be acute and life-threatening. Even water, when consumed in excess, can be toxic.

While the influence of nutrition on human health and disease was discovered only as recently as the late 19th century, food itself has long been of fundamental importance to human survival. Where food is plentiful, populations are healthy; they grow and prosper. Conversely, where it is in short supply, people suffer from hunger and disease. For years scientists in the field of nutrition have worked to identify which nutrients and quantities of nutrients are required for optimum human health. That information, in turn, has served a crucial role in guiding the dietary decisions of individuals and societies around the globe.

CHAPTER 1

FOOD AND THE HUMAN BODY

Nutrition is the process by which substances in food are used to provide energy for the full range of physical and mental activities that characterize human life. It is also the process by which substances in food are transformed into body tissues, such as muscle and fat. These actions are essential to human health, and their importance in people's daily lives is reflected in everything from nutrition labels on food products to the vast numbers of people worldwide who are affected by malnutrition or excess weight gain.

The study of human nutrition is interdisciplinary in character, involving not only physiology, biochemistry, and molecular biology but also fields such as psychology and anthropology, which explore the influence of attitudes, beliefs, preferences, and cultural traditions on food choices. Human nutrition further touches on economics and political science as the world community recognizes and responds to, on the one hand, the suffering and death caused by malnutrition and, on the other, the costs to individuals and societies of obesity. The ultimate goal of nutritional science is to promote optimal health and reduce the risk of chronic diseases such as cardiovascular disease and cancer as well as to prevent classic nutritional deficiency diseases such as kwashiorkor and pellagra.

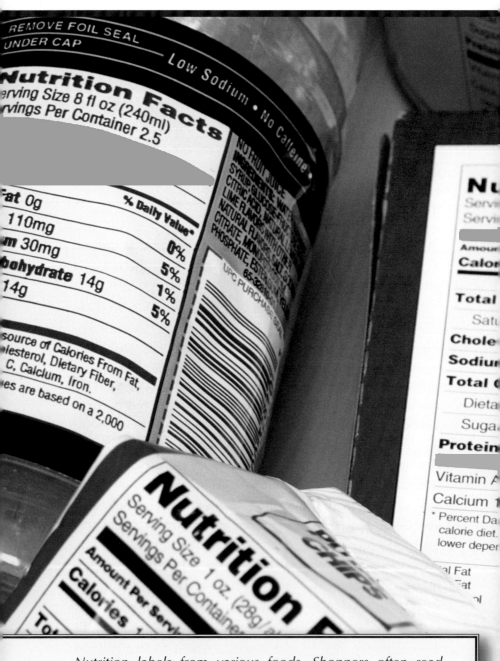

Nutrition labels from various foods. Shoppers often read the information regarding nutrients on food packaging to better understand what they're putting into their bodies.
C. Sherburne/PhotoLink/Photodisc/Getty Images

Scientists have long been interested in the chemical composition of foods. Humans require organic material in their diet, in addition to water and minerals. This organic matter must be sufficient in quantity to satisfy caloric, or energy, requirements. Within certain limits, carbohydrate, fat, and protein may be used interchangeably for this purpose. In addition, however, humans have nutritional requirements for specific organic compounds, including essential fatty acids, essential amino acids, and vitamins. While the nutritional requirements of humans are similar to other animal species, they are not necessarily identical. For example, humans require vitamin C (ascorbic acid), whereas rats do not.

Modern understanding of food and human nutrition emerged from studies of energy, respiration, and metabolism that were conducted primarily in the 19th and 20th centuries. In the 20th century, for example, studies showed that the energy produced by the metabolism of foodstuffs in an animal equals that produced by the combustion of these foodstuffs outside the body. After these studies, basal metabolic rate (BMR), a measure of body metabolism based on the amount of oxygen an individual takes in while at rest, was developed and used in the diagnosis of certain diseases, and data relating the composition of foodstuffs to their value as sources of metabolic energy were obtained.

Ultimately, nutrition came to be viewed as a way to supply the body with sufficient sources of energy and specific substances that it cannot synthesize. Comparative animal studies, which were of practical importance in the discovery of some vitamins, led also to the general observation that the specific nutrient requirements of animals are consequences of a slow evolutionary deterioration in which synthetic abilities are lost through changes or mutations in hereditary material.

THE UTILIZATION OF FOOD BY THE BODY

The human body can be thought of as an engine that releases the energy present in the foods that it digests. This energy is utilized partly for the mechanical work performed by the muscles and in the secretory processes and partly for the work necessary to maintain the body's structure and functions. The performance of work is associated with the production of heat; heat loss is controlled so as to keep body temperature within a narrow range. Unlike other engines, however, the human body is continually breaking down (catabolizing) and building up (anabolizing) its component parts. Foods supply nutrients essential to the manufacture of the new material and provide energy needed for the chemical reactions involved.

CALORIES AND KILOCALORIES: ENERGY SUPPLY

Carbohydrate, fat, and protein are, to a large extent, interchangeable as sources of energy. Typically, the energy provided by food is measured in kilocalories, or calories. One kilocalorie is equal to 1,000 gram-calories (or small calories), a measure of heat energy. However, in common parlance, kilocalories are referred to as "calories." In other words, a 2,000-calorie diet actually has 2,000 kilocalories of potential energy. One kilocalorie is the amount of heat energy required to raise one kilogram of water from 14.5 to 15.5 °C at one atmosphere of pressure. Another unit of energy widely used is the joule, which measures energy in terms of mechanical work. One joule is the energy expended when one kilogram is moved a distance of one metre by a force of one newton. The relatively higher levels of energy in human nutrition are more likely to be measured in kilojoules (1 kilojoule =

10^3 joules) or megajoules (1 megajoule = 10^6 joules). One kilocalorie is equivalent to 4.184 kilojoules.

The energy present in food can be determined directly by measuring the output of heat when the food is burned (oxidized) in a bomb calorimeter. However, the human body is not as efficient as a calorimeter, and some potential energy is lost during digestion and metabolism. Corrected physiological values for the heats of combustion of the three energy-yielding nutrients, rounded to whole numbers, are as follows: carbohydrate, 4 kilocalories (17 kilojoules) per gram; protein, 4 kilocalories (17 kilojoules) per gram; and fat, 9 kilocalories (38 kilojoules) per gram. Beverage alcohol (ethyl alcohol) also yields energy—7 kilocalories (29 kilojoules) per gram—although it is not essential in the diet.

A rice vendor in India weighs his product at market. Rice is a staple source of nutrition in some countries, where more carbohydrates are consumed than proteins. Noah Seelam/ AFP/Getty Images

Vitamins, minerals, water, and other food constituents have no energy value, although many of them participate in energy-releasing processes in the body.

The energy provided by a well-digested food can be estimated if the gram amounts of energy-yielding substances (non-fibre carbohydrate, fat, protein, and alcohol) in that food are known. For example, a slice of white bread containing 12 grams of carbohydrate, 2 grams of protein, and 1 gram of fat supplies 67 kilocalories (280 kilojoules) of energy. Food composition tables and food labels provide useful data for evaluating energy and nutrient intake of an individual diet. Most foods provide a mixture of energy-supplying nutrients, along with vitamins, minerals, water, and other substances. Two notable exceptions are table sugar and vegetable oil, which are virtually pure carbohydrate (sucrose) and fat, respectively.

Throughout most of the world, protein supplies between 8 and 16 percent of the energy in the diet, although there are wide variations in the proportions of fat and carbohydrate in different populations. In more prosperous communities about 12 to 15 percent of energy is typically derived from protein, 30 to 40 percent from fat, and 50 to 60 percent from carbohydrate. On the other hand, in many poorer agricultural societies, where cereals comprise the bulk of the diet, carbohydrate provides an even larger percentage of energy, with protein and fat providing less. The human body is remarkably adaptable and can survive, and even thrive, on widely divergent diets. However, different dietary patterns are associated with particular health consequences.

BMR AND REE: ENERGY BALANCE

Energy is needed not only when a person is physically active but even when the body is lying motionless. Depending on an individual's level of physical activity, between 50 and 80 percent of the energy expended each day is devoted to basic metabolic processes (basal metabolism), which enable the body to stay warm, breathe, pump blood, and conduct numerous physiological and biosynthetic activities, including synthesis of new tissue in growing children and in pregnant and lactating women. Digestion and subsequent processing of food by the body also uses energy and produces heat. This phenomenon, known as the thermic effect of food (or diet-induced thermogenesis), accounts for about 10 percent of daily energy expenditure, varying somewhat with the composition of the diet and prior dietary practices. Adaptive thermogenesis, another small but important component of energy expenditure, reflects alterations in metabolism due to changes in ambient temperature, hormone production, emotional stress, or other factors. Finally, the most variable component in energy expenditure is physical activity, which includes exercise and other voluntary activities as well as involuntary activities such as fidgeting, shivering, and maintaining posture. Physical activity accounts for 20 to 40 percent of the total energy expenditure, even less in a very sedentary person and more in someone who is extremely active.

Basal or resting energy expenditure is correlated primarily with lean body mass (fat-free mass and essential fat, excluding storage fat), which is the metabolically active tissue in the body. At rest, organs such as the liver, brain, heart, and kidney have the highest metabolic activity and, therefore, the highest need for energy, while muscle and bone require less energy, and body fat even less. Besides body composition, other factors affecting basal metabolism include age, sex, body temperature, and thyroid hormone levels.

The basal metabolic rate (BMR), a precisely defined measure of the energy expenditure necessary to support life, is determined under controlled and standardized conditions—shortly after awakening in the morning, at least 12 hours after the last meal, and with a comfortable room temperature. Because of practical considerations, the BMR is rarely measured; the resting energy expenditure (REE) is determined under less stringent conditions, with the individual resting comfortably about 2 to 4 hours after a meal. In practice, the BMR and REE differ by no more than 10 percent—the REE is usually slightly higher—and the terms are used interchangeably.

Energy expenditure can be assessed by direct calorimetry, or measurement of heat dissipated from the body, which employs apparatuses such as water-cooled garments or insulated chambers large enough to accommodate a person. However, energy expenditure is usually measured by the less cumbersome techniques of indirect calorimetry, in which heat produced by the body is calculated from measurements of oxygen inhaled, carbon dioxide exhaled, and urinary nitrogen excreted. The BMR (in kilocalories per day) can be roughly estimated using the following formula: BMR = 70 × (body weight in kilograms)34.

The energy costs of various activities have been measured. While resting may require as little as 1 kilocalorie per minute, strenuous work may demand 10 times that much. Mental activity, though it may seem taxing, has no appreciable effect on energy requirement. A 154-pound (70-kg) man, whose REE over the course of a day might be 1,750 kilocalories, could expend a total of 2,400 kilocalories on a very sedentary day and up to 4,000 kilocalories on a very active day. A 121-pound (55-kg) woman, whose daily resting energy expenditure might be 1,350 kilocalories, could use from 1,850 to more than 3,000 total kilocalories, depending on level of activity.

The law of conservation of energy applies: If one takes in more energy than is expended, over time one will gain weight;

insufficient energy intake results in weight loss, as the body taps its energy stores to provide for immediate needs. Excess food energy is stored in small amounts as glycogen, a short-term storage form of carbohydrate in muscle and liver, and as fat, the body's main energy reserve found in adipose tissue. Adipose tissue is mostly fat (about 87 percent), but it also contains some protein and water. In order to lose one pound (454 grams) of adipose tissue, an energy deficit of about 3,500 kilocalories (14.6 megajoules) is required.

BODY MASS, BODY FAT, AND BODY WATER

The human body consists of materials similar to those found in foods; however, the relative proportions differ, according to genetic dictates as well as to the unique life experience of the individual. The body of a healthy lean man is composed of roughly 62 percent water, 16 percent fat, 16 percent protein, 6 percent minerals, and less than 1 percent carbohydrate, along with very small amounts of vitamins and other miscellaneous substances. Females usually carry more fat (about 22 percent in a healthy lean woman) and slightly less of the other components than do males of comparable weight.

The body's different compartments—lean body mass, body fat, and body water—are constantly adjusting to changes in the internal and external environment so that a state of dynamic equilibrium (homeostasis) is maintained. Tissues in the body are continuously being broken down and built up at varying rates. For example, the epithelial cells lining the digestive tract are replaced at a dizzying speed of every three or four days, while the life span of red blood cells is 120 days, and connective tissue is renewed over the course of several years.

Although estimates of the percentage of body fat can be made by direct inspection, this approach is imprecise. Body

BODY MASS INDEX

Body mass index (BMI) is an estimate of total body fat. BMI is defined as weight in kilograms divided by the square of the height in metres: weight $\div$ height^2 = BMI. This number, which is central to determining whether an individual is clinically defined as obese, parallels fatness but is not a direct measure of body fat. BMI is less sensitive than using a skinfold caliper or other method to measure body fat indirectly.

Interpretation of BMI numbers is based on weight status groupings, such as underweight, healthy weight, overweight, and obese, that are adjusted for age and sex. For all adults over age 20, BMI numbers correlate to the same weight status designations. For example, a BMI for adult women and men between 18.5 and 24.9 is considered healthy. A BMI lower than 18.5 is considered underweight, whereas a BMI between 25.0 and 29.9 equates with overweight and 30.0 and above with obesity. Definitions of overweight and obesity are more difficult to quantify for children, whose BMI changes with age.

fat can be measured indirectly using fairly precise but costly methods, such as underwater weighing, total body potassium counting, and dual-energy X-ray absorptiometry (DXA). However, more practical, albeit less accurate, methods are often used, such as anthropometry, in which subcutaneous fat at various sites is measured using skinfold calipers; bioelectrical impedance, in which resistance to a low-intensity electrical current is used to estimate body fat; and near infrared interactance, in which an infrared light aimed at the biceps is used to assess fat and protein interaction. Direct measurement of the body's various compartments can only be performed on cadavers.

The composition of the body tends to change in somewhat predictable ways over the course of a lifetime—during the growing years, in pregnancy and lactation, and as one ages—with corresponding changes in nutrient needs during different phases of the life cycle. Regular physical exercise can help attenuate the age-related loss of lean tissue and increase in body fat.

DIETARY AND NUTRIENT RECOMMENDATIONS

Notions of what constitutes a healthful diet vary with geography and custom as well as with changing times and an evolving understanding of nutrition. In the past, people had to live almost entirely on food that was locally produced. With industrialization and globalization, however, food can now be transported over long distances. Researchers must be careful in making generalizations about a national diet from a relatively small sample of the population; the poor cannot afford to eat the same diet as the rich, and many countries have large immigrant groups with their own distinctive food patterns. Even within a culture, some people abstain on moral or religious grounds from eating certain foods. In general, persons living in more affluent countries eat more meat and other animal products. By comparison, the diets of those living in poorer, agricultural countries rely primarily on cereals in the form of wheat flour, white rice, or corn, with animal products providing less than 10 percent of energy. Another difference between cultures is the extent to which dairy products are consumed. The Chinese, for example, obtain about 2 percent of their energy from dairy products. In contrast, in Pakistan dairy products contribute almost 10 percent of energy. Among Western diets, the lowest in saturated fat is the so-called Mediterranean diet. In the

1950s it was found that Europeans living in rural areas near the Mediterranean Sea had a greater life expectancy than those living elsewhere in Europe, despite poor medical services and a lower standard of living. The traditional diet of Mediterranean peoples is low in animal products; instead, olive oil is a major source of monounsaturated fat. Also, tomatoes and green leafy vegetables, which are regularly consumed in large quantities in the region, contain a variety of antioxidant compounds that are thought to be healthful.

DIETARY GUIDELINES

Following the publication of dietary goals for the Nordic countries in 1968 and for the United States in 1977, dietary goals and guidelines have been set forth by a number of countries and revised periodically as a way of translating scientific recommendations into simple and practical dietary suggestions. These authoritative statements—some published by scientific bodies and some by government agencies—aim to promote long-term health and to prevent or reduce the chances of developing chronic and degenerative diseases. Although the guidelines of different countries may vary in important ways, most recent dietary recommendations include variations on the following fundamental themes: eat a variety of foods; perform regular physical activity and maintain a healthy weight; limit consumption of saturated fat, trans fat, sugar, salt (more specifically, sodium), and alcohol; and emphasize vegetables, fruits, and whole grains.

FOOD GUIDE PYRAMIDS AND OTHER AIDS

Different formats for dietary goals and guidelines have been developed over the years as educational tools, grouping foods of similar nutrient content together to help facilitate the selection of a balanced diet. In the United States, the four food-group plan of the 1950s—which suggested a milk group, a meat group, a fruit and vegetable group, and a breads and cereals group as a basic diet—was replaced in 1992 by the five major food groups of the Food Guide Pyramid. This innovative visual display was introduced by the United States Department of Agriculture (USDA) as a tool for helping the public cultivate a daily pattern of

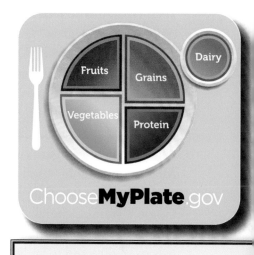

The MyPlate chart, which replaced the food pyramid guide in the United States in 2011. USDA

wise food choices, ranging from liberal consumption of grain products, as represented in the broad base of the pyramid, to sparing use of fats, oils, and sugary foods, as represented in the apex.

Subsequently, similar devices were developed for particular cultural and ethnic food patterns such as Asian, Latin American, Mediterranean, and even vegetarian diets—all emphasizing grains, vegetables, and fruits. While an adaptation of the 1992 USDA pyramid was used by Mexico, Chile, the Philippines, and Panama, a rainbow was used by Canada, a square by Zimbabwe, plates by Australia and the United Kingdom, a bean pot by Guatemala, the number 6 by Japan, and a pagoda by South Korea and China.

In the early 21st century, many countries altered the pictorial representation of their food guides. For example, in

2005 Japan introduced a spinning-top food guide that essentially was an inverted version of the U.S. pyramid graphic. That same year, the USDA released new dietary guidelines and redesigned its original Food Guide Pyramid, which was known as MyPyramid and featured colourful vertical stripes of varying widths to reflect the relative proportions of different food groups. Similar to Japan's spinning-top graphic, which depicted a figure running on the top's upper level, the MyPyramid graphic used a figure climbing steps to illustrate the importance of daily exercise. Unlike the original Food Guide Pyramid, the abstract geometry of MyPyramid did not offer specific dietary guidance at a glance; rather, individuals were directed to an interactive Web site for customized eating plans based on their age, sex, and activity level.

In 2011 the USDA abandoned MyPyramid and introduced MyPlate, which divided the four basic food groups (fruits, grains, protein, and vegetables) into sections on a plate, with the size of each section representing the relative dietary proportions of each food group. A small circle shown at the edge of the plate was used to illustrate the dietary inclusion and proportion of dairy products. Unlike MyPyramid, MyPlate did not include an exercise component, nor did it include a section for fats and oils. The two were similar, however, in that the guidance they offered was nonspecific and was supported by a Web site.

ADAPTING GUIDELINES TO CULTURE

Dietary guidelines have been largely the province of more affluent countries, where correcting imbalances due to overconsumption and inappropriate food choices has been key. Not until 1989 were proposals for dietary guidelines published from the perspective of low-income countries, such as India, where the primary nutrition problems stemmed from the lack of opportunity to acquire or consume needed

Health Canada | Santé Canada | *Your health and safety... our priority.* | *Votre santé et votre sécurité... notre priorité.*

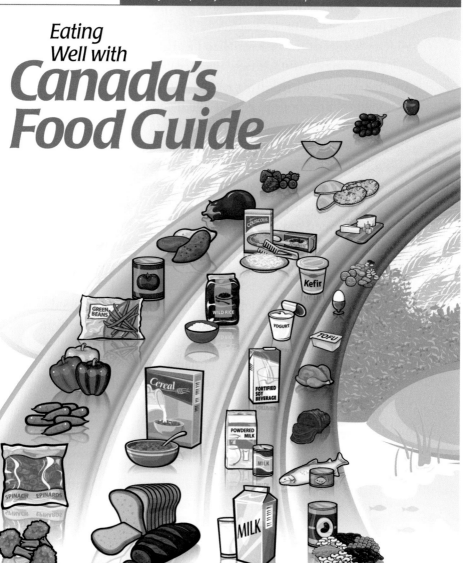

The cover of Canada's food guide, Eating Well with Canada's Food Guide, *featuring the food rainbow.* Health Canada, 2012. Reproduced with the permission of the Minister of Health, 2012.

food. But even in such countries, there was a growing risk of obesity and chronic disease among the small but increasing number of affluent people who had adopted some of the dietary habits of the industrialized world.

For example, the Chinese Dietary Guidelines, published by the Chinese Nutrition Society in 1997, made recommendations for that part of the population dealing with nutritional diseases such as those resulting from iodine and vitamin A deficiencies, for people in some remote areas where there was a lack of food, as well as for the urban population coping with changing lifestyle, dietary excess, and increasing rates of chronic disease. The Food Guide Pagoda, a graphic display intended to help Chinese consumers put the dietary recommendations into practice, rested on the traditional cereal-based Chinese diet. Those who could not tolerate fresh milk were encouraged to consume yogurt or other dairy products as a source of calcium. Unlike dietary recommendations in Western countries, the pagoda did not include sugar, as sugar consumption by the Chinese was quite low; however, children and adolescents in particular were cautioned to limit sugar intake because of the risk of dental caries.

NUTRIENT RECOMMENDATIONS

The relatively simple dietary guidelines discussed above provide guidance for meal planning. Standards for evaluating the adequacy of specific nutrients in an individual diet or the diet of a population require more detailed and quantitative recommendations. Nutrient recommendations are usually determined by scientific bodies within a country at the behest of government agencies. The World Health Organization and other agencies of the United Nations have also issued reports on nutrients and food components. The Recommended Dietary Allowances (RDAs), first published by the U.S.

National Academy of Sciences in 1941 and revised every few years until 1989, established dietary standards for evaluating nutritional intakes of populations and for planning food supplies. The RDAs reflected the best scientific judgment of the time in setting amounts of different nutrients adequate to meet the nutritional needs of most healthy people.

DIETARY REFERENCE INTAKES

During the 1990s a paradigm shift took place as scientists from the United States and Canada joined forces in an ambitious multiyear project to reframe dietary standards for the two countries. In the revised approach, known as the Dietary Reference Intakes (DRIs), classic indicators of deficiency, such as scurvy and beriberi, were considered an insufficient basis for recommendations. Where warranted by a sufficient research base, the guidelines rely on indicators with broader significance, those that might reflect a decreased risk of chronic diseases such as osteoporosis, heart disease, hypertension, or cancer. DRIs are intended to help individuals plan a healthful diet as well as avoid consuming too much of a nutrient. The comprehensive approach of the DRIs has served as a model for other countries. DRI reports were published in 1997 and in 2004, with subsequent updates on specific nutrients.

The collective term "Dietary Reference Intakes" encompasses four categories of reference values. The Estimated Average Requirement (EAR) is the intake level for a nutrient at which the needs of 50 percent of the population will be met. Because the needs of the other half of the population will not be met by this amount, the EAR is increased by about 20 percent to arrive at the RDA. The RDA is the average daily dietary intake level sufficient to meet the nutrient requirement of nearly all (97 to 98 percent) healthy persons in a particular life stage. When the EAR, and thus the RDA, cannot be set due to insufficient scientific evidence, another parameter, the Adequate Intake (AI), is given, based on estimates of intake levels of healthy populations. Lastly, the Tolerable Upper Intake Level (UL) is the highest level of a daily nutrient intake that will most likely present no risk of adverse health effects in almost all individuals in the general population.

Nutrition information is commonly displayed on food labels, but this information is generally simplified to avoid confusion. Because only one nutrient reference value is listed, and because sex and age categories usually are not taken into consideration, the amount chosen is generally the highest RDA value. In the United States, for example, the Daily Values, determined by the Food and Drug Administration, are generally based on RDA values published in 1968. The different food components are listed on the food label as a percentage of their Daily Values.

Confidence that a desirable level of intake is reasonable for a particular group of people can be bolstered by multiple lines of evidence pointing in the same direction, an understanding of the function of the nutrient and how it is handled by the body, and a comprehensive theoretical model with strong statistical underpinnings. Of critical importance in estimating nutrient requirements is explicitly defining the criterion that the specified level of intake is intended to satisfy. Approaches that use different definitions of adequacy are not comparable. For example, it is one thing to prevent clinical impairment of bodily function (basal requirement), which does not necessarily require any reserves of the nutrient, but it is another to consider an amount that will provide desirable reserves (normative requirement) in the body. Yet another approach attempts to evaluate a nutrient intake conducive to optimal health, even if an amount is required beyond that normally obtainable in food—possibly necessitating the use of supplements. Furthermore, determining upper levels of safe intake requires evidence of a different sort. These issues are extremely complex, and the scientists who collaborate to set nutrient recommendations face exceptional challenges in their attempts to reach consensus.

NUTRITION THROUGHOUT THE LIFE CYCLE

Nutritional needs and concerns vary during different stages of life. These variations range from the level of caloric input to the type of nutrient needed. So, while growing children have increased caloric demands relative to infants and require increased amounts of calcium for their growing bones, infants have unique nutrient requirements, and those that are breast-fed may need to have their diets supplemented with specific vitamins. Likewise, nutrition in adults, even those of the same age, may vary. For example, pregnant women have their own set of nutritional requirements, which differ from those of other adults, and these requirements vary further, depending on a pregnant woman's health and whether she is underweight or overweight or has a healthy weight.

PREGNANCY AND LACTATION

A woman's nutritional status before and during pregnancy affects not only her own health but also the health and development of her baby. If a woman is underweight before becoming pregnant or fails to gain sufficient weight during pregnancy, her chance of having a premature or low-birth-weight infant is increased.

Overweight women, on the other hand, have a high risk of complications during pregnancy, such as high blood pressure (hypertension) and gestational diabetes, and of having a poorly developed infant or one with birth defects. Weight loss during pregnancy is never recommended. Recommended weight gain during pregnancy is 25 to 35 pounds (11.5 to 16 kg) for a woman of normal weight—slightly more for an underweight woman and slightly less for an overweight woman.

At critical periods in the development of specific organs and tissues, there is increased vulnerability to nutrient deficiencies, nutrient excesses, or toxins. For example, excess vitamin A taken early in pregnancy can cause brain malformations in the fetus. One important medical advance of the late 20th century was the recognition that a generous intake of folic acid (also called folate or folacin) in early pregnancy reduces the risk of birth defects, specifically neural tube defects such as spina bifida and anencephaly (partial or complete absence of the brain), which involve spinal cord damage and varying degrees of paralysis, if not death. For this reason, supplementation with 400 micrograms (µg; 1 µg = 0.000001 gram) of folic acid is recommended for all women who have a chance of becoming pregnant. Good food sources of folic acid include green leafy vegetables, citrus fruit and juice, beans and other legumes, whole grains, fortified breakfast cereals, and liver.

Overall nutritional requirements increase with pregnancy. In the second and third trimesters, pregnant women need additional food energy—about 300 kilocalories above nonpregnant needs. Most additional nutrient needs can be met by selecting food wisely, but an iron supplement (30 mg per day) is usually recommended during the second and third trimesters, in addition to a folic acid supplement throughout pregnancy. Other key nutrients of particular concern are protein, vitamin D, calcium, and zinc.

Heavy alcohol consumption or "binge drinking" during pregnancy can cause fetal alcohol syndrome, a condition with irreversible mental and physical retardation. Even lighter social drinking during pregnancy may result in milder damage—growth retardation, behavioral or learning abnormalities, or motor impairments—sometimes described as fetal alcohol effects. Until a completely safe level of intake can be determined, pregnant women are advised not to drink at all, especially during the first trimester. Caffeine consumption is usually limited as a precautionary measure, and cigarette smoking is not advised under any circumstances. Limiting intake of certain fish, such as swordfish and shark, which may be contaminated with methylmercury, is also recommended.

An extra 500 kilocalories of food per day is needed to meet the energy demands of lactation. Because pregnancy depletes maternal iron stores, iron supplementation during lactation may be advised. Breast-fed infants may be sensitive to the constituents and flavours of foods and beverages consumed by the mother. In general, lactating women are advised to consume little, if any, alcohol.

INFANCY, CHILDHOOD, AND ADOLESCENCE

Breast-fed infants, in general, have fewer infections and a reduced chance of developing allergies and food intolerances. For these and other reasons, breast-feeding is strongly recommended for at least the first four to six months of life. However, if a woman is unable to breast-feed or chooses not to, infant formulas (altered forms of cow's milk) can provide safe and adequate nourishment for an infant. Goat's milk, evaporated milk, and sweetened condensed milk are inappropriate for infants.

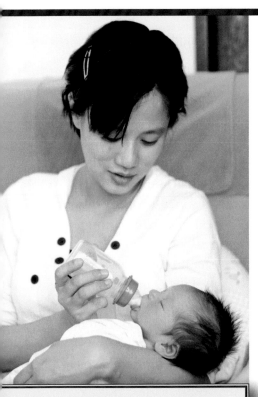

A young mother bottle-feeds her child. Infant formulas can be a nutritious alternative to a mother's breast milk, provided they are prepared properly. Lawren/Flickr/ Getty Images

Soy formulas and hydrolyzed protein formulas can be used if a milk allergy is suspected. In developing countries with poor sanitation, over-diluted formulas or those prepared with contaminated water can cause malnutrition and infection, resulting in diarrhea, dehydration, and even death. Breast-fed infants may need supplements of iron and vitamin D during the first six months of life and fluoride after six months. A vitamin B12 supplement is advised for breast-fed infants whose mothers are strict vegetarians (vegans).

Solid foods, starting with iron-fortified infant cereals, can be introduced between four and six months to meet nutrient needs that breast milk or infant formulas can no longer supply alone. Other foods can be introduced gradually, one every few days. Infants should not be given honey (which may contain bacteria that can cause botulism), foods that are too salty or sweet, foods that may cause choking, or large amounts of fruit juice.

Starting at one year of age, whole cow's milk can be an excellent source of nutrients for children. However, because cow's milk is associated with gastrointestinal blood loss, iron deficiency, and an allergic response in some young infants, some medical societies do not recommend giving unmodified whole cow's milk to children less than one year old. Low-fat or nonfat milk is inappropriate for children less than two years of age.

The rapid growth rate of infancy slows down in early childhood. During childhood—but not before the age of two—a gradual transition to lower-fat foods is recommended, along with regular exercise. Establishing healthful practices in childhood will reduce the risk of childhood obesity as well as obesity in adulthood and related chronic diseases (e.g., heart disease, diabetes, and high blood pressure).

Vegetarian children can be well nourished but care is needed for them to receive sufficient energy (calories), good-quality protein, vitamins B12 and D, and the minerals iron, zinc, and calcium. It is difficult for children who do not drink milk to obtain enough calcium from their food, and supplements may be required. Because of possible toxicity, iron supplements should be taken only under medical supervision.

A small percentage of school-age children who have difficulty sitting still and paying attention are diagnosed with attention-deficit/hyperactivity disorder (ADHD). Studies have found no convincing evidence that ADHD is caused by sugar or food additives in the diet or that symptoms can be alleviated by eliminating these substances.

Because of unusual eating practices, skipped meals, and concerns about body image, many teenagers, especially girls, have a less than optimal diet. Teenage girls, in particular, need to take special care to obtain adequate amounts of calcium so that bones can be properly mineralized. Iron-deficiency anemia is a concern not only for teenage girls, who lose iron periodically in menstrual blood, but also for teenage boys.

ADULTHOOD

No matter which nutritional and health practices are followed, the body continues to age, and there appears to be a strong genetic component to life expectancy. Nevertheless, healthful dietary practices and habits such as limited alcohol use, avoidance of tobacco products, and regular physical activity can help reduce the chance of premature death and increase the chance of vitality in the older years. For the most part, a diet that is beneficial for adults in general is also beneficial for people as they age, taking into account possible changes in energy needs.

In elderly people, common problems that contribute to inadequate nutrition are tooth loss, decreased sense of taste and smell, and a sense of isolation—all of which result in decreased food intake and weight loss. The elderly may have gastrointestinal ailments, such as poor absorption of vitamin B12, and digestion difficulties, such as constipation. Inadequate fluid intake may lead to dehydration. Nutritional deficiency may further compromise declining immune function. Prescription and over-the-counter drugs may interact with nutrients and exacerbate the nutritional deficits of the elderly. In addition, decreasing physical activity, loss of muscle tissue, and increasing body fat are associated with type 2 diabetes, hypertension, and risk of cardiovascular disease and other diseases. Older people, especially those with reduced sun exposure or low intakes of fatty fish or vitamin D-fortified food, may need supplemental vitamin D to help preserve bone mass. Adequate calcium intake and weight-bearing exercise are also important, but these measures cannot completely stop the decline in bone density with age that makes both men and women vulnerable to bone fractures (due to osteoporosis), which could leave them bedridden and could even be life-threatening.

Treatment with various bone-conserving drugs has been found to be effective in slowing bone loss. Staying physically fit as one ages can improve strength and balance, thereby preventing falls, contributing to overall health, and reducing the impact of aging.

There is evidence that intake of the antioxidants vitamin C, vitamin E, and beta-carotene as well as the mineral zinc may slow the progression of age-related macular degeneration, a leading cause of blindness in people older than 65 years. Two carotenoids, lutein and zeaxanthin, also are being studied for their possible role in protecting against age-related vision loss. Research suggests that the dietary supplement glucosamine, a substance that occurs naturally in the body and contributes to cartilage formation, may be useful in lessening the pain and disability of osteoarthritis. Aerobic exercise and strength training, as well as losing excess weight, also may provide some relief from arthritis pain.

Preliminary evidence suggests that fish oil, rich in omega-3 fatty acids, helps reduce the joint inflammation of rheumatoid arthritis. Fish oil also reduces blood clotting and exerts other effects that may protect the heart and blood vessels. However, in large quantities it may contribute to hemorrhagic stroke and have other undesirable side effects. Although consumption of fish once or twice a week may be beneficial, supplementation with fish oil capsules is advised only with medical supervision.

Elevated blood levels of the amino acid homocysteine have been associated with an increased risk of cardiovascular disease and with Alzheimer's disease, the most common form of dementia; certain B vitamins, particularly folic acid, may be effective in lowering homocysteine levels. High concentrations of aluminum in the brains of persons with Alzheimer's disease are most likely a result of the disease and not a cause, as

ELSIE WIDDOWSON

(b. Oct. 21, 1906, London, Eng.—d. June 14, 2000, Cambridge, Eng.)

English nutritionist Elsie Widdowson contributed to fundamental investigations of the chemical composition of foods—work that helped guide the British government's World War II food-rationing program.

Widdowson received bachelor's (1928) and doctoral (1931) degrees in chemistry from Imperial College, London. Following completion of her doctorate, she spent a year at the Courtauld Institute of Biochemistry at Middlesex Hospital before moving to King's College of Household and Social Science in 1933. It was there, while studying dietetics, that she met Robert A. McCance, her longtime research partner. She accompanied him to Cambridge when he accepted a position there in 1938.

Widdowson and McCance documented the nutritional content of thousands of foods, eventually compiling their findings in the *The Chemical Composition of Foods* (1940), which became a classic in the field of nutrition and was revised several times. Spurred by the British government's concerns about the effects of the heavy rationing necessitated by the outbreak of World War II, the pair did extensive research into the effects of dietary deprivation, eventually determining that a basic diet of bread, potatoes, and cabbage was sufficient. Later research led them to advocate the fortification of food (notably bread) with iron, vitamins, and calcium.

Widdowson remained a member of the research staff at the University of Cambridge until 1972. She served as president of the Nutrition Society (1977–80), the Neonatal Society (1978–81), and the British Nutrition Foundation (1986–96) and was elected to the Royal Society (1976). Widdowson was made a Commander of the British Empire (CBE) in 1979 and a Companion of Honour in 1993. In 1999 the Elsie Widdowson Laboratory for human nutrition research was dedicated at Cambridge.

correspondingly high levels of aluminum are not found in blood and hair. There is ongoing research into the possible value of dietary supplements for the normal memory problems that beset healthy older people.

Eating a healthful diet, obtaining sufficient sleep, avoiding smoking, keeping physically fit, and maintaining an active mind are among the practices that may increase not only life expectancy but also the chance of a full and productive life in one's later years. The so-called free-radical theory of aging—the notion that aging is accelerated by highly reactive substances that damage cellular components, and that intake of various antioxidants can repair free-radical damage and thereby slow aging—has generated much interest and is a promising area of research, but it has not been scientifically established. On the contrary, the life spans of various mammalian species have not been extended significantly by antioxidant therapy. Ongoing studies are investigating whether the consumption of 30 percent fewer calories (undernutrition, not malnutrition) slows aging and age-related disease and extends life spans in nonhuman primates. There is no evidence that severe energy restriction would extend the human life span beyond its current maximum of 115 to 120 years.

CHAPTER 2

THE ESSENTIAL NUTRIENTS

The six classes of nutrients found in foods are carbohydrates, lipids (mostly fats and oils), proteins, vitamins, minerals, and water. Carbohydrates, lipids, and proteins constitute the bulk of the diet, amounting together to about just over one pound (500 grams) per day in actual weight. These macronutrients provide raw materials for tissue building and maintenance as well as fuel to run the myriad physiological and metabolic activities that sustain life. In contrast are the micronutrients, which are not themselves energy sources but facilitate metabolic processes throughout the body: vitamins, of which humans need about 300 mg per day in the diet, and minerals, of which about 20 grams per day are needed. The last nutrient category is water, which provides the medium in which all the body's metabolic processes occur.

A nutrient is considered "essential" if it must be taken in from outside the body—in most cases, from food. Although these nutrients are separated into categories in the following sections for purposes of discussion, one should keep in mind that nutrients work in collaboration with one another in the body, not as isolated entities. Discussed briefly here, vitamins are covered in detail elsewhere in the book.

CARBOHYDRATES

Carbohydrates, which are composed of carbon, hydrogen, and oxygen, are the major supplier of energy to the body, providing 4 kilocalories per gram. In most carbohydrates, the elements hydrogen and oxygen are present in the same 2:1 ratio as in water, thus "carbo" (for carbon) and "hydrate" (for water).

GLUCOSE

The simple carbohydrate glucose is the principal fuel used by the brain and nervous system and by red blood cells. Muscle and other body cells can also use glucose for energy, although fat is often used for this purpose. Because a steady supply of glucose is so critical to cells, blood glucose is maintained within a relatively narrow range through the action of various hormones, mainly insulin, which directs the flow of glucose into cells, and glucagon and epinephrine, which retrieve glucose from storage. The body stores a small amount of glucose as glycogen, a complex branched form of carbohydrate, in liver and muscle tissue, and this can be broken down to glucose and used as an energy source during short periods (a few hours) of fasting or during times of intense physical activity or stress. If blood glucose falls below normal (hypoglycemia), weakness and dizziness may result. Elevated blood glucose (hyperglycemia), as can occur in diabetes, is also dangerous and cannot be left untreated.

Glucose can be made in the body from most types of carbohydrate and from protein, although protein is usually an expensive source of energy. Some minimal amount of carbohydrate is required in the diet—at least 50 to 100 grams a day. This not only spares protein but also ensures that fats are completely metabolized and prevents a condition known as ketosis, the accumulation of products of fat breakdown, called ketones, in the body. Although there are great variations in the quantity and type of carbohydrates eaten throughout the world, most diets contain more than enough.

SIR NORMAN HAWORTH

(b. March 19, 1883, Chorley, Lancashire, Eng.—d. March 19, 1950, Birmingham)

British chemist Sir Walter Norman Haworth was a cowinner, with the Swiss chemist Paul Karrer, of the 1937 Nobel Prize for Chemistry for his work in determining the chemical structures of carbohydrates and vitamin C.

Haworth graduated from the University of Manchester in 1906 and received a Ph.D. degree from the University of Göttingen in 1910. He taught at the University of St. Andrews (1912–20) and the University of Durham (1920–25). Haworth joined the faculty of St. Andrews University in 1912. While at St. Andrews, he worked with the British chemists Sir James Irvine and Thomas Purdie in the study of carbohydrates, including sugars, starch, and cellulose. They found that sugars have a ringlike, rather than a straight-line, arrangement of their carbon atoms; these ringlike representations of sugar molecules have come to be known as Haworth formulas. Haworth's book *The Constitution of Sugars* (1929) became a standard text.

In 1925 Haworth became director of the chemistry department at the University of Birmingham, where he turned to the study of vitamin C, which is structurally similar to simple sugars. In 1934, with the British chemist Sir Edmund Hirst, he succeeded in synthesizing the vitamin, the first to be artificially produced. This accomplishment not only constituted a valuable addition to knowledge of organic chemistry but also made possible the cheap production of vitamin C (or ascorbic acid, as Haworth called it) for medical purposes. Haworth was knighted in 1947.

OTHER SUGARS AND STARCH

The simplest carbohydrates are sugars, which give many foods their sweet taste but at the same time provide food

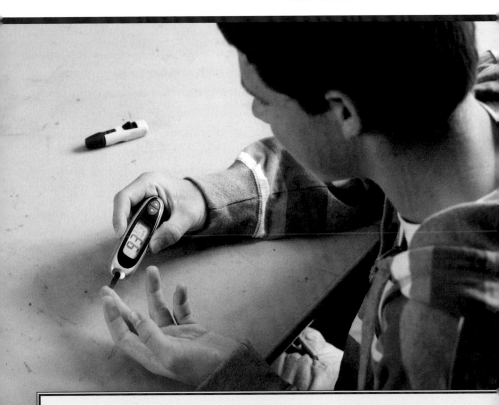

A young man testing his blood sugar. Levels of the hormone insulin help keep a steady supply of glucose available in the human body. iStockphoto/Thinkstock

for bacteria in the mouth, thus contributing to dental decay. Sugars in the diet are monosaccharides, which contain one sugar or saccharide unit, and disaccharides, which contain two saccharide units linked together. Monosaccharides of nutritional importance are glucose, fructose, and galactose; disaccharides include sucrose (table sugar), lactose (milk sugar), and maltose. A slightly more complex type of carbohydrate is the oligosaccharide (e.g., raffinose and stachyose), which contains three to 10 saccharide units. These compounds, which are found in beans and other legumes and cannot be digested well by humans, account for the gas-producing effects of these foods.

Larger and more complex storage forms of carbohydrate are the polysaccharides, which consist of long chains of glucose units. Starch, the most important polysaccharide in the human diet—found in grains, legumes, potatoes, and other vegetables—is made up of mainly straight glucose chains (amylose) or mainly branching chains (amylopectin). Finally, nondigestible polysaccharides known as dietary fibre are found in plant foods such as grains, fruits, vegetables, legumes, seeds, and nuts.

In order to be utilized by the body, all complex carbohydrates must be broken down into simple sugars, which, in turn, must be broken down into monosaccharides—a feat, accomplished by enzymes, that starts in the mouth and ends in the small intestine, where most absorption takes place. Each dissacharide is split into single units by a specific enzyme; for example, the enzyme lactase breaks down lactose into its constituent monosaccharides, glucose and galactose. In much of the world's population, lactase activity declines during childhood and adolescence, which leads to an inability to digest lactose adequately. This inherited trait, called lactose intolerance, results in gastrointestinal discomfort and diarrhea if too much lactose is consumed. Those who have retained the ability to digest dairy products efficiently in adulthood are primarily of northern European ancestry.

DIETARY FIBRE

Dietary fibre, the structural parts of plants, cannot be digested by the human intestine because the necessary enzymes are lacking. Even though these nondigestible compounds pass through the gut unchanged (except for a small percentage that is fermented by bacteria in the large intestine), they nevertheless contribute to good health.

Insoluble fibre does not dissolve in water and provides bulk, or roughage, that helps with bowel function (regularity)

Foods such as oats and fruit provide the human body with soluble fibre, which helps rid the body of harmful cholesterol buildup in the bloodstream. Michael Rosenfeld/ Photographer's Choice/Getty Images

and accelerates the exit from the body of potentially carcinogenic or otherwise harmful substances in food. Types of insoluble fibre are cellulose, most hemicelluloses, and lignin (a phenolic polymer, not a carbohydrate). Major food sources of insoluble fibre are whole grain breads and cereals, wheat bran, and vegetables.

Soluble fibre, which dissolves or swells in water, slows down the transit time of food through the gut (an undesirable effect) but also helps lower blood cholesterol levels (a desirable effect). Types of soluble fibre are gums, pectins, some hemicelluloses, and mucilages;

fruits (especially citrus fruits and apples), oats, barley, and legumes are major food sources.

Both soluble and insoluble fibre help delay glucose absorption, thus ensuring a slower and more even supply of blood glucose. Dietary fibre is thought to provide important protection against some gastrointestinal diseases and to reduce the risk of other chronic diseases as well.

LIPIDS

Lipids also contain carbon, hydrogen, and oxygen but in a different configuration, having considerably fewer oxygen atoms than are found in carbohydrates. Lipids are soluble in organic solvents (such as acetone or ether) and insoluble in water, a property that is readily seen when an oil-and-vinegar salad dressing separates quickly upon standing. The lipids of nutritional importance are triglycerides (fats and oils), phospholipids (e.g., lecithin), and sterols (e.g., cholesterol).

In a person's diet, lipids transport the four fat-soluble vitamins (vitamins A, D, E, and K) and assist in their absorption in the small intestine. They also carry with them substances that impart sensory appeal and palatability to food and provide satiety value, the feeling of being full and satisfied after eating a meal. Fats in the diet are a more concentrated form of energy than carbohydrates and have an energy yield of 9 kilocalories per gram. Adipose (fatty) tissue in the fat depots of the body serves as an energy reserve as well as helping to insulate the body and cushion the internal organs.

TRIGLYCERIDES

The major lipids in food and stored in the body as fat are the triglycerides, which consist of three fatty acids attached to a backbone of glycerol (an alcohol). Fatty acids are essentially hydrocarbon chains with a carboxylic acid group (COOH) at one end, the alpha (α) end, and a methyl group (CH3) at the other, omega (ω), end. They are classified as saturated or unsaturated according to their chemical structure. A point of unsaturation indicates a double bond between two carbon atoms, rather than the full complement of hydrogen atoms that is present in saturated fatty acids. A monounsaturated fatty acid has one point of unsaturation, while a polyunsaturated fatty acid has two or more.

Fatty acids found in the human diet and in body tissues range from a chain length of 4 carbons to 22 or more, each chain having an even number of carbon atoms. Of particular importance for humans are the 18-carbon polyunsaturated fatty acids alpha-linolenic acid (an omega-3 fatty acid) and linoleic acid (an omega-6 fatty acid); these are known as essential fatty acids because they are required in small amounts in the diet. The omega designations (also referred to as n-3 and n-6) indicate the location of the first double bond from the methyl end of the fatty acid. Other fatty acids can be synthesized in the body and are therefore not essential in the diet.

About a tablespoon daily of an ordinary vegetable oil such as safflower or corn oil or a varied diet that includes grains, nuts, seeds, and vegetables can fulfill the essential fatty acid requirement. Essential fatty acids are needed for the formation of cell membranes and the synthesis of hormone-like compounds called eicosanoids (e.g., prostaglandins, thromboxanes, and leukotrienes), which are important regulators of blood pressure, blood clotting, and the immune response. The consumption of fish once or twice a week provides an additional source of omega-3 fatty acids that appears to be healthful.

A fat consisting largely of saturated fatty acids, especially long-chain fatty acids, tends to be solid at room temperature; if unsaturated fatty acids predominate, the fat is liquid at room temperature. Fats and oils usually contain mixtures of fatty acids, although the type of fatty acid in greatest concentration typically gives the food its characteristics. Butter and other animal fats are primarily saturated; olive and canola oils, monounsaturated; and fish, corn, safflower, soybean, and sunflower oils, polyunsaturated. Although plant oils tend to be largely unsaturated, there are notable exceptions, such as coconut fat, which is highly saturated but nevertheless semiliquid at room temperature because its fatty acids are of medium chain length (8 to 14 carbons long).

Saturated fats tend to be more stable than unsaturated ones. The food industry takes advantage of this property during hydrogenation, in which hydrogen molecules are added to a point of unsaturation, thereby making the fatty acid more stable and resistant to rancidity (oxidation) as well as more solid and spreadable (as in margarine). However, a result of the hydrogenation process is a change in the shape of some unsaturated fatty acids from a configuration known as cis to that known as trans. Trans-fatty acids, which behave more like saturated fatty acids, have undesirable health consequences.

PHOSPHOLIPIDS

A phospholipid is similar to a triglyceride except that it contains a phosphate group and a nitrogen-containing compound such as choline instead of one of the fatty acids. In food, phospholipids are natural emulsifiers, allowing fat and water to mix, and they are used as food additives for this purpose. In the body, phospholipids allow fats to be suspended in fluids such as blood, and they enable lipids to move across cell membranes from one watery compartment to another. The phospholipid lecithin is plentiful in foods such as egg yolks, liver, wheat germ, and peanuts. However, the liver is able to synthesize all the lecithin the body needs if sufficient choline is present in the diet.

STEROLS

Sterols are unique among lipids in that they have a multiple-ring structure. The well-known sterol cholesterol is found only in foods of animal origin—meat, egg yolk, fish, poultry, and dairy products. Organ meats (e.g., liver, kidney) and egg yolks have the most cholesterol, while muscle meats and cheeses have less. There are a number of sterols in shellfish but not as much cholesterol as was once thought. Cholesterol is essential to the structure of cell membranes and is also used to make other important sterols in the body, among them the sex hormones, adrenal hormones, bile acids, and vitamin D. However, cholesterol can be synthesized in the liver, so there is no need to consume it in the diet.

Cholesterol-containing deposits may build up in the walls of arteries, leading to a condition known as atherosclerosis, which contributes to myocardial infarction (heart attack) and stroke. Furthermore, because elevated levels of blood cholesterol, especially the form known as low-density lipoprotein (LDL) cholesterol, have been associated with an increased risk of cardiovascular disease, a limited intake of saturated fat—particularly medium-chain saturated fatty acids, which act to raise LDL cholesterol levels—is advised. Trans-fatty acids also raise LDL cholesterol, while monounsaturated and polyunsaturated (cis) fats tend to lower LDL cholesterol levels. Because of the body's feedback mechanisms, dietary cholesterol has only a minor influence on blood cholesterol in most people;

however, since some individuals respond strongly to cholesterol in the diet, a restricted intake is often advised, especially for those at risk of heart disease.

PROTEINS

Proteins, like carbohydrates and fats, contain carbon, hydrogen, and oxygen, but they also contain nitrogen, a component of the amino chemical group (NH_2), and in some cases sulfur. Proteins serve as the basic structural material of the body as well as being biochemical catalysts and regulators of genes. Aside from water, protein

A bodybuilder drinking a shake made from whey, which is a form of protein. Ingesting increased amounts of protein helps athletes gain and keep muscle tone and strength. Paul Kane/Getty Images

constitutes the major part of muscles, bones, internal organs, and the skin, nails, and hair. Protein is also an important part of cell membranes and blood (e.g., hemoglobin). Enzymes, which catalyze chemical reactions in the body, are also protein, as are antibodies, collagen in connective tissue, and many hormones, such as insulin.

Tissues throughout the body require ongoing repair and replacement, and thus the body's protein is turning over constantly, being broken down and then resynthesized as needed. Tissue proteins are in a dynamic equilibrium with proteins in the blood, with input from proteins in the diet and losses through urine, feces, and skin. In a healthy adult, adjustments are made so that the amount of protein lost is in balance with the amount of protein ingested. However, during periods of rapid growth, pregnancy and lactation, or recuperation after illness or depletion, the body is in positive nitrogen balance, as more protein is being retained than excreted. The opposite is true during illness or wasting, when there is negative nitrogen balance as more tissue is being broken down than synthesized.

AMINO ACIDS

The proteins in food—such as albumin in egg white, casein in dairy products, and gluten in wheat—are broken down during digestion into constituent amino acids, which, when absorbed, contribute to the body's metabolic pool. Amino acids are then joined via peptide linkages to assemble specific proteins, as directed by the genetic material and in response to the body's needs at the time. Each gene makes one or more proteins, each with a unique sequence of amino acids and precise three-dimensional configuration. Amino acids are also required for the synthesis of other important nonprotein compounds, such as peptide hormones, some neurotransmitters, and creatine.

Food contains approximately 20 common amino acids, 9 of which are considered essential, or indispensable, for humans; i.e., they cannot be synthesized by the body or cannot be synthesized in sufficient quantities and therefore must be taken in the diet. The essential amino acids for humans are histidine, isoleucine, leucine, lysine, methionine, phenylalanine, threonine, tryptophan, and valine. Conditionally indispensable amino acids include arginine, cysteine, and tyrosine, which may need to be provided under special circumstances, such as in premature infants or in people with liver disease, because of impaired conversion from precursors.

The relative proportions of different amino acids vary from food to food. Foods of animal origin—meat, fish, eggs, and dairy products—are sources of good quality, or complete, protein; i.e., their essential amino acid patterns are similar to human needs for protein. (Gelatin, which lacks the amino acid tryptophan, is an exception.) Individual foods of plant origin, with the exception of soybeans, are lower quality, or incomplete, protein sources. Lysine, methionine, and tryptophan are the primary limiting amino acids; i.e., they are in smallest supply and therefore limit the amount of protein that can be synthesized. However, a varied vegetarian diet can readily fulfill human protein requirements if the protein-containing foods are balanced such that their essential amino acids complement each other. For example, legumes such as beans are high in lysine and low in methionine, while grains have complementary strengths and weaknesses. Thus, if beans and rice are eaten over the course of a day, their joint amino acid patterns will supplement each other and provide a higher quality protein than would either food alone.

Traditional food patterns in native cultures have made good use of protein complementarity. However, careful balancing of plant proteins is necessary only for those whose protein intake is marginal or inadequate. In affluent populations, where protein intake is greatly in excess of needs, obtaining sufficient good quality protein is usually only a concern for young children who are not provided with animal proteins.

PROTEIN INTAKE

The World Health Organization recommends a daily intake of 0.75 gram of good quality protein per kilogram of body weight for adults of both sexes. Thus, a 154-pound (70-kg) man would need 52.5 grams of protein, and a 121 pound (55-kg) woman would need about 41 grams of protein. This recommendation, based on nitrogen balance studies, assumes an adequate energy intake. Infants, children, and pregnant and lactating women have additional protein needs to support synthesis of new tissue or milk production. Protein requirements of endurance athletes and bodybuilders may be slightly higher than those of sedentary individuals, but this has no practical significance because athletes typically consume much more protein than they need.

Protein consumed in excess of the body's needs is degraded; the nitrogen is excreted as urea, and the remaining keto acids are used for energy, providing 4 kilocalories per gram, or are converted to carbohydrate or fat. During conditions of fasting, starvation, or insufficient dietary intake of protein, lean tissue is broken down to supply amino acids for vital body functions. Persistent protein inadequacy results in suboptimal metabolic function with increased risk of infection and disease.

VITAMINS

Vitamins—which are discussed in detail in chapter three—are organic compounds found in very small amounts in food and required for normal functioning—indeed, for survival. Humans are able to synthesize certain vitamins to some extent. For example, vitamin D is produced when the skin is exposed to sunlight; niacin can be synthesized from the amino acid tryptophan; and vitamin K and biotin are synthesized by bacteria living in the gut. However, in general, humans depend on their diet to supply vitamins. When a vitamin is in short supply or is not able to be utilized properly, a specific deficiency syndrome results. When the deficient vitamin is resupplied before irreversible damage occurs, the signs and symptoms are reversed. The amounts of vitamins in foods and the amounts required on a daily basis are measured in milligrams and micrograms.

Vitamin nomenclature is somewhat complex, with chemical names gradually replacing the original letter designations created in the era of vitamin discovery during the first half of the 20th century. Nomenclature is further complicated by the recognition that vitamins are parts of families with, in some cases, multiple active forms. Some vitamins are found in foods in precursor forms that must be activated in the body before they can properly fulfill their function. For example, beta(β)-carotene, found in plants, is converted to vitamin A in the body.

The 13 vitamins known to be required by humans are categorized into two groups according to their solubility. The four fat-soluble vitamins (soluble in nonpolar solvents) are vitamins A, D, E, and K. Although now known to behave as a hormone, the activated form of vitamin D, vitamin D hormone (calcitriol), is still grouped with the vitamins as well. The nine water-soluble vitamins (soluble in polar solvents) are vitamin C and the eight B-complex vitamins: thiamin, riboflavin, niacin, vitamin B6, folic acid, vitamin B12, pantothenic acid, and biotin. Choline is a vitamin-like dietary component that is clearly required for normal metabolism but that can be synthesized by the body. Although choline may be necessary in the diet of premature infants and possibly of those with certain medical conditions, it has not been established as essential in the human diet throughout life.

Different vitamins are more or less susceptible to destruction by environmental conditions and chemical agents. For example, thiamin is especially vulnerable to prolonged heating, riboflavin to ultraviolet or fluorescent light, and vitamin C to oxidation (as when a piece of fruit is cut open and the vitamin is exposed to air). In general, water-soluble vitamins are more easily destroyed during cooking than are fat-soluble vitamins.

Vitamins synthesized in the laboratory are the same molecules as those extracted from food, and they cannot be distinguished by the body. However, various forms of a vitamin are not necessarily equivalent. In the particular case of vitamin E, supplements labeled d-α-tocopherol (or "natural") generally contain more vitamin E activity than those labeled dl-α-tocopherol. Vitamins in food have a distinct advantage over vitamins in supplement form because they come associated with other substances that may be beneficial, and there is also less potential for toxicity. Nutritional supplements cannot substitute for a healthful diet.

MINERALS

Unlike the complex organic compounds (carbohydrates, lipids, proteins, vitamins) discussed in previous sections, minerals are simple inorganic elements—often in the form of salts in the body—that are not themselves metabolized, nor are they a source of energy. Minerals constitute about 4 to 6 percent of body weight—about one-half as calcium and one-quarter as phosphorus (phosphates), the remainder being made up of the other essential minerals that must be derived from the diet. Minerals not only impart hardness to bones and teeth but also function broadly in metabolism—e.g., as electrolytes controlling the movement of water in and out of cells, as components of enzyme systems, and as constituents of many organic molecules.

As nutrients, minerals are traditionally divided into two groups according to the amounts present in and needed by the body. The major minerals (macrominerals)—those required in amounts of 100 mg or more per day—are calcium, phosphorus (phosphates), magnesium, sulfur, sodium, chloride, and potassium. The trace elements (microminerals or trace minerals), required in much smaller amounts of about 15 mg per day or less, include iron, zinc, copper, manganese, iodine (iodide), selenium, fluoride, molybdenum, chromium, and cobalt (as part of the vitamin B12 molecule). Fluoride is considered a beneficial nutrient because of its role in protecting against dental caries, although an essential function in the strict sense has not been established in human nutrition.

The term ultratrace elements is sometimes used to describe minerals that are found in the diet in extremely small quantities (micrograms each day) and are present in human tissue as well; these include arsenic, boron, nickel, silicon, and vanadium. Despite demonstrated roles in experimental animals, the exact function of these and other ultratrace elements (e.g., tin, lithium, aluminum) in human tissues and indeed their importance for human health are uncertain.

Minerals have diverse functions, including muscle contraction, nerve transmission, blood clotting, immunity, the maintenance of blood pressure, and growth and development. The major minerals, with the exception of sulfur, typically occur in the body in ionic (charged) form: sodium, potassium, magnesium, and calcium as positive ions (cations) and chloride and phosphates as negative ions (anions). Mineral salts dissolved in body fluids help regulate fluid balance, osmotic pressure, and acid-base balance.

Sulfur, too, has important functions in ionic forms (such as sulfate), but much of the body's sulfur is nonionic, serving as an integral part of certain organic molecules, such as the B vitamins thiamin, biotin, and pantothenic acid and the amino acids methionine, cysteine, and cystine. Other mineral elements that are constituents of organic compounds include iron, which is part of hemoglobin (the oxygen-carrying protein in red blood cells), and iodine, a component of thyroid hormones, which help regulate body metabolism. Additionally, phosphate groups are found in many organic molecules, such as phospholipids in cell membranes, genetic material (DNA and RNA), and the high-energy molecule adenosine triphosphate (ATP).

The levels of different minerals in foods are influenced by growing conditions (e.g., soil and water composition) as well as by how the food is processed. Minerals are not destroyed during food preparation; in fact, a food can be burned completely and the minerals (ash) will remain unchanged. However, minerals can be lost by leaching into cooking water that is subsequently discarded.

Many factors influence mineral absorption and thus availability to the body. In general, minerals are better absorbed from animal foods than from plant foods. The latter contain fibre and other substances that interfere with absorption. Phytic acid, found principally in cereal grains and legumes, can form complexes with some minerals and make them insoluble and thereby indigestible. Only a small percentage of the calcium in spinach is absorbed because spinach also contains large amounts of oxalic acid, which binds calcium. Some minerals, particularly those of a similar size and charge, compete with each other for absorption. For example, iron supplementation may reduce zinc absorption, while excessive intakes of zinc can interfere with copper absorption. On the other hand, the absorption of iron from plants (nonheme iron) is enhanced when vitamin C is simultaneously present in the diet, and calcium absorption is improved by adequate amounts of vitamin D. Another key factor that influences mineral absorption is the physiological need for the mineral at the time.

Unlike many vitamins, which have a broader safety range, minerals can be toxic if taken in doses not far above recommended levels. This is particularly true for the trace elements, such as iron and copper. Accidental ingestion of iron supplements has been a major cause of fatal poisoning in young children.

WATER

Although often overlooked as a nutrient, water (H_2O) is actually the most critical nutrient of all. Humans can survive weeks without food but only a matter of days without water. Water provides the medium in which nutrients and waste products are transported throughout the body and the myriad biochemical reactions of metabolism occur. Water allows for temperature regulation, the maintenance of blood pressure and blood volume, the structure of large molecules, and the rigidity of body tissues. It also acts as a solvent, a lubricant (as in joints), and a protective cushion (as inside the eyes and in spinal fluid and amniotic fluid). The flow of water in and out of cells is precisely controlled by shifting electrolyte concentrations on either side of the cell membrane. Potassium, magnesium, phosphate, and sulfate are primarily intracellular electrolytes; sodium and chloride are major extracellular ones.

Drinking water during a bike ride or other form of exercise is important because physical activity depletes fluids at a quicker pace, and may cause dehydration. iStockphoto/Thinkstock

Water makes up about 50 to 70 percent of body weight, approximately 60 percent in healthy adults and an even higher percentage in children. Because lean tissue is about three-quarters water, and fatty tissue is only about one-fifth water, body composition—the amount of fat in particular—determines the percentage of body water. In general, men have more lean tissue than women, and therefore a higher percentage of their body weight is water.

Water is consumed not only as water itself and as a constituent of other beverages but also as a major component of many foods, particularly fruits and vegetables, which may contain from 85 to 95 percent water. Water also is manufactured in the body as an end product of metabolism. About 2.6 quarts (about 2.5 litres) of water are turned over daily, with water excretion (primarily in urine, water vapour from lungs, sweat loss from skin, and feces) balancing intake from all sources.

Because water requirements vary with climate, level of activity, dietary composition, and other factors, there is no one recommendation for daily water intake. However, adults typically need at least 8 cups (2 litres) of water a day, from all sources. Thirst is not reliable as a register for dehydration, which typically occurs before the body is prompted to replace fluid. Therefore, water intake is advised throughout the day, especially with increased sweat loss in hot climates or during vigorous physical activity, during illness, or in a dehydrating situation such as an airplane flight.

CHAPTER 3

THE VITAMINS

Vitamins are distinct in several ways from other biologically important compounds such as proteins, carbohydrates, and lipids. Although these latter substances are indispensable for proper bodily functions, almost all of them can be synthesized by animals in adequate quantities. Vitamins, on the other hand, generally cannot be synthesized in amounts sufficient to meet bodily needs and therefore must be obtained from the diet or from some synthetic source. For this reason, vitamins are called essential nutrients. Vitamins also differ from the other biological compounds in that relatively small quantities are needed to complete their functions. In general these functions are of a catalytic or regulatory nature, facilitating or controlling vital chemical reactions in the body's cells. If a vitamin is absent from the diet or is not properly absorbed by the body, a specific deficiency disease may develop.

BIOLOGICAL SIGNIFICANCE OF VITAMINS

Unlike the macronutrients, vitamins do not serve as an energy source for the body or provide raw materials for tissue building. Rather, they assist in energy-yielding reactions and facilitate metabolic and physiologic processes throughout the body. Vitamin A, for example, is required for embryonic development, growth, reproduction,

One tablet daily, with food.

ment Facts

Amount Per Serving	% Daily Value	
3500 IU	70%	Niacin
		Vitamin B6
90 mg	150%	Folic Acid
400 IU	100%	Vitamin F
45 IU	150%	Biotin
20 mcg	25%	Panto
1.2 mg	80%	Calc
1.7 mg	100%	Ma

a carotene)

CHILD RESISTANT
"SEALED for YOUR

EACH OF CHILDREN

The label on a bottle of vitamins, showing the percentage of daily recommended allowances for individual vitamins and minerals contained in the supplement.
© iStockphoto.com/kledge

proper immune function, and the integrity of epithelial cells, in addition to its role in vision. The B vitamins function as coenzymes that assist in energy metabolism; folic acid (folate), one of the B vitamins, helps protect against birth defects in the early stages of pregnancy. Vitamin C plays a role in building connective tissue as well as being an antioxidant that helps protect against damage by reactive molecules (free radicals). Now considered to be a hormone, vitamin D is involved in calcium and phosphorus homeostasis and bone metabolism. Vitamin E, another antioxidant, protects against free radical damage in lipid systems, and vitamin K plays a key role in blood clotting. Although vitamins are often discussed individually, many of their functions are interrelated, and a deficiency of one can influence the function of another.

The solubility of a vitamin influences the way it is absorbed, transported, stored, and excreted by the body as well as where it is found in foods. With the exception of vitamin B12, which is supplied by only foods of animal origin, the water-soluble vitamins are synthesized by plants and found in both plant and animal foods. Strict vegetarians (vegans), who eat no foods of animal origin, are therefore at risk of vitamin B12 deficiency. Fat-soluble vitamins, on the other hand, are found in association with fats and oils in foods and in the body and typically require protein carriers for transport through the water-filled compartments of the body.

Water-soluble vitamins are not appreciably stored in the body (except for vitamin B12) and thus must be consumed regularly in the diet. If taken in excess they are readily excreted in the urine, although there is potential toxicity even with water-soluble vitamins; especially noteworthy in this regard is vitamin B6. Because fat-soluble vitamins are stored in the liver and fatty tissue, they do not necessarily have to be taken in daily, so long as average intakes over time—weeks, months, or even years—meet the body's needs. However, the fact that these vitamins can be stored increases the possibility of toxicity if very large doses are taken. This is particularly of concern with vitamins A and D, which can be toxic if taken in excess. Under certain circumstances, pharmacological ("megadose") levels of some vitamins—many times higher than the amount typically found in food—have accepted medical uses. Niacin, for example, is used to lower blood cholesterol levels; vitamin D is used to treat psoriasis; and pharmacological derivatives of vitamin A are used to treat acne and other skin conditions as well as to diminish skin wrinkling. However, consumption of vitamins or other dietary supplements in amounts significantly in excess of recommended levels is not advised without medical supervision.

DISCOVERY AND ORIGINAL DESIGNATION

Some of the first evidence for the existence of vitamins emerged in the late 19th century, with the work of Dutch physician and pathologist Christiaan Eijkman. In 1890 a nerve disease (polyneuritis) broke out among his

English biochemist Sir Frederick Gowland Hopkins. Science & Society Picture Library/Getty Images

SIR FREDERICK GOWLAND HOPKINS

(b. June 20, 1861, Eastbourne, East Sussex, Eng.—d. May 16, 1947, Cambridge)

British biochemist Sir Frederick Gowland Hopkins received (with Christiaan Eijkman) the 1929 Nobel Prize for Physiology or Medicine for the discovery of essential nutrient factors—now known as vitamins—needed in animal diets to maintain health.

In 1901 Hopkins discovered the amino acid tryptophan, isolated it from protein, and eventually (1906–07) showed that it and certain other amino acids (known as essential amino acids) cannot be manufactured by certain animals from other nutrients and must be supplied in the diet. Noticing that rats failed to grow on a diet of artificial milk but grew rapidly when a small quantity of cow's milk was added to their daily ration, Hopkins realized that no animal can live on a mixture of pure protein, fat, and carbohydrate, even when mineral salts are added, and described the missing factors—later called vitamins—as "accessory" factors or substances.

In 1907 Hopkins and Sir Walter Fletcher laid the foundations for a modern understanding of the chemistry of muscular contraction when they demonstrated that working muscle accumulates lactic acid. Fifteen years later, Hopkins isolated from living tissue the tripeptide (three amino acids linked in sequence) glutathione and showed that it is vital to the utilization of oxygen by the cell.

Hopkins spent most of his career at Cambridge University (1898–1943). He was knighted in 1925 and received many other honours, including the presidency of the Royal Society (1930) and the Order of Merit (1935).

laboratory chickens. He noticed that the disease bore a striking resemblance to the polyneuritis occurring in the nutritional disorder beriberi, and he was eventually (1897) able to show that the condition was caused by feeding the chickens a diet of polished, rather than unpolished, rice. In 1906–07 British biochemist Sir Frederick Gowland Hopkins observed that animals cannot synthesize certain amino acids and concluded that macronutrients and salts could not by themselves support growth.

In 1912—the same year that Hopkins published his findings about the missing nutrients, which he described as "accessory" factors or substances—a Polish scientist, Casimir Funk, demonstrated that polyneuritis produced in pigeons fed on polished rice could be cured by supplementing the birds' diet with a concentrate made from rice bran, a component of the outer husk that was removed from rice during polishing. Funk proposed that the polyneuritis arose because of a lack in the birds' diet of a vital factor (now known to be thiamin) that could be found in rice bran. Funk believed that some human diseases, particularly beriberi, scurvy, and pellagra, also were caused by deficiencies of factors of the same chemical type. Because each of these factors had a nitrogen-containing component known as an amine, he called the compounds "vital amines," a term that he later shortened to "vitamines." The final *e* was dropped later when it was discovered that not

Casimir Funk, the scientist whose study of rice-fed pigeons led to the connection between vitamin deficiencies and certain diseases in humans. Herb Scharfman/Time & Life Pictures/Getty Images

all of the vitamins contain nitrogen and, therefore, not all are amines.

In 1913 American researcher Elmer McCollum divided vitamins into two groups: "fat-soluble A" and "water-soluble B." As claims for the discovery of other vitamins multiplied, researchers called the new substances C, D, and so on. Later it was realized that the water-soluble growth factor, vitamin B, was not a single entity but at least two—only one of which prevented polyneuritis in pigeons. The factor required by pigeons was called vitamin B1, and the other factor, essential for rats, was designated vitamin B2. As chemical structures of the vitamins became known, they were also given chemical names, e.g., thiamin for vitamin B1 and riboflavin for vitamin B2. (See the table in the Appendix.)

REGULATORY ROLE

The vitamins regulate reactions that occur in metabolism, in contrast to macronutrients (e.g., fats, carbohydrates, proteins), which are the compounds utilized in the reactions regulated by the vitamins. Absence of a vitamin blocks one or more specific metabolic reactions in a cell and eventually may disrupt the metabolic balance within a cell and in the entire organism as well.

With the exception of vitamin C, all of the water-soluble vitamins have a catalytic function, acting as coenzymes of enzymes that function in energy transfer or in the metabolism of fats, carbohydrates, and proteins. The metabolic importance of the water-soluble vitamins is reflected by their presence in most plant and animal tissues involved in metabolism.

Some of the fat-soluble vitamins form part of the structure of biological membranes or assist in maintaining the integrity (and therefore, indirectly, the function) of membranes. Some fat-soluble vitamins also may function at the genetic level by controlling the synthesis of certain enzymes. Unlike the water-soluble ones, fat-soluble vitamins are necessary for specific functions in highly differentiated and specialized tissues. Therefore, their distribution in nature tends to be more selective than that of the water-soluble vitamins.

SOURCES

Vitamins, which are found in all living organisms either because they are synthesized in the organism or are acquired from the environment, are not distributed equally throughout nature. Some are absent from certain tissues or species; for example, beta-carotene, which can be converted to vitamin A, is synthesized in plant tissues but not in animal tissues. On the other hand, vitamins A and D3 (cholecalciferol) occur only in animal tissues. Both plants and animals are important natural vitamin sources for humans. Since vitamins are not distributed equally in foodstuffs, the more restricted the diet of an individual, the more likely it is that he or she will lack adequate amounts of one or more vitamins. Food sources of vitamin

D are limited, but it can be synthesized in the skin through ultraviolet radiation (from the sun). Therefore, with adequate exposure to sunlight, the dietary intake of vitamin D is of little significance.

All vitamins can be either synthesized or produced commercially from food sources and are available for human consumption in pharmaceutical preparations. Commercial processing of food (e.g., milling of grains) frequently destroys or removes considerable amounts of vitamins. In most such instances, however, the vitamins are replaced by chemical methods. Some foods are fortified with vitamins not normally present in them (e.g., vitamin D is added to milk). Loss of vitamins may also occur when food is cooked. For instance, heat destroys vitamin A, and water-soluble vitamins may be extracted from food to water and lost. Certain vitamins (e.g., B vitamins, vitamin K) can be synthesized by microorganisms normally present in the intestines of some animals. However, the microorganisms usually do not supply the host animal with an adequate quantity of a vitamin.

REQUIREMENTS IN LIVING THINGS

Vitamin requirements vary according to species, and the amount of a vitamin required by a specific organism is difficult to determine because of the numerous factors (e.g., genetic variation, relative proportions of other dietary constituents, environmental stresses). Although there is not uniform agreement concerning the human requirements of vitamins, recommended daily vitamin intakes are sufficiently high to account for individual variation and normal environmental stresses.

A number of interrelationships exist among vitamins and between vitamins and other dietary constituents. The interactions may be synergistic (i.e., cooperative) or

antagonistic, reflecting, for example, overlapping metabolic roles (of the B vitamins in particular), protective
roles (e.g., vitamins A and E), or structural dependency
(e.g., cobalt in the vitamin B12 molecule).

RESULTS OF DEFICIENCIES

Inadequate intake of a specific vitamin results in a characteristic deficiency disease (hypovitaminosis), the severity
of which depends upon the degree of vitamin deprivation.
Symptoms may be specific (e.g., functional night blindness
of vitamin A deficiency) or nonspecific (e.g., loss of appetite, failure to grow). All symptoms for a specific deficiency
disease may not appear. In addition, the nature of the symptoms may vary with the species. Some effects of vitamin
deficiencies cannot be reversed by adding the vitamin to
the diet, especially if damage to nonregenerative tissue (e.g.,
cornea of the eye, nerve tissue, calcified bone) has occurred.

A vitamin deficiency may be primary (or dietary), in
which case the dietary intake is lower than the normal
requirement of the vitamin. A secondary (or conditioned)
deficiency may occur (even though the dietary intake
is adequate) if a preexisting disease or state of stress is
present (e.g., malabsorption of food from the intestine,
chronic alcoholism, repeated pregnancies and lactation).

EVOLUTION OF VITAMIN-DEPENDENT ORGANISMS

Evolution of metabolic processes in primitive forms of life
required the development of enzyme systems to catalyze
the complex sequences of chemical reactions involved in
metabolism. In the beginning, the environment presumably could supply all the necessary compounds (including
the vitamin coenzymes). Eventually, these compounds
were synthesized within an organism. As higher forms of

life evolved, however, the ability to synthesize certain of these vitamin coenzymes was gradually lost.

Since higher plants show no requirements for vitamins or other growth factors, it is assumed that they retain the ability to synthesize them. Among insects, however, niacin, thiamin, riboflavin, vitamin B6, vitamin C, and pantothenic acid are required by a few groups. All vertebrates, including humans, require dietary sources of vitamin A, vitamin D, thiamin, riboflavin, vitamin B6, and pantothenic acid. Some vertebrates, particularly the more highly evolved ones, have additional requirements for other vitamins.

THE WATER-SOLUBLE VITAMINS

Water-soluble vitamins are distinguished from fat-soluble vitamins by their need for replenishment in the body. They include vitamin C (ascorbic acid) and the B vitamins: thiamin (vitamin B1), riboflavin (vitamin B2), vitamin B6, niacin (nicotinic acid), vitamin B12, folic acid, pantothenic acid, and biotin. These relatively simple molecules contain the elements carbon, hydrogen, and oxygen. Some also contain nitrogen, sulfur, or cobalt.

BASIC PROPERTIES

Although the vitamins included in this classification are all water-soluble, the degree to which they dissolve in water is variable. This property influences the route of absorption, their excretion, and their degree of tissue storage and distinguishes them from fat-soluble vitamins, which are handled and stored differently by the body.

The water-soluble vitamins, inactive in their so-called free states, must be activated to their coenzyme forms. Addition of phosphate groups occurs in the activation of thiamin, riboflavin, and vitamin B6, while a shift in structure activates biotin, and formation of a complex between the free vitamin and parts of other molecules is involved in the activation of niacin, pantothenic acid, folic acid, and vitamin B12. After an active coenzyme is formed, it must combine with the proper protein component (called an apoenzyme) before enzyme-catalyzed reactions can occur.

FUNCTIONS

The B-vitamin coenzymes function in enzyme systems that transfer certain groups between molecules. As a result, specific proteins, fats, and carbohydrates are formed and may be utilized to produce body tissues or to store or release energy. The pantothenic acid coenzyme functions in the tricarboxylic acid cycle (also called the Krebs, or citric acid, cycle), which interconnects carbohydrate, fat, and protein metabolism. This coenzyme (coenzyme A) acts at the hub of these reactions and thus is an important molecule in controlling the interconversion of fats, proteins, and carbohydrates and their conversion into metabolic energy. Thiamin and vitamin B6 coenzymes control the conversion of carbohydrates and proteins respectively into metabolic energy during the citric acid cycle. Niacin and riboflavin coenzymes facilitate the transfer of hydrogen ions or electrons (negatively charged particles), which occurs during the reactions of the tricarboxylic acid cycle. All of these coenzymes also function in transfer reactions that are involved in the synthesis of structural compounds. These reactions are not part of the tricarboxylic acid cycle.

Although vitamin C participates in some enzyme-catalyzed reactions, it has not yet been established that the vitamin is a coenzyme. Its function probably is related to its properties as a strong reducing agent (i.e., it readily gives electrons to other molecules).

METABOLISM

The water-soluble vitamins are absorbed in the animal intestine, pass directly to the blood, and are carried to the tissues in which they will be utilized. Vitamin B12 requires a substance known as intrinsic factor in order to be absorbed.

Some of the B vitamins can occur in forms that cannot be used by an animal. Most of the niacin in some cereal grains (wheat, corn, rice, barley, bran), for example, is bound to another substance, forming a complex called niacytin that cannot be absorbed in the animal intestine. Biotin can be bound by the protein avidin, which is found in raw egg white. This complex also cannot be absorbed or broken down by digestive-tract enzymes, and thus the biotin cannot be utilized. In animal products (e.g., meat), biotin, vitamin B6, and folic acid are bound to other molecules to form complexes or conjugated molecules. Although none is active in the complex form, the three vitamins normally are released from the bound forms by the enzymes of the intestinal tract (for biotin and vitamin B6) or in the tissues (for folic acid) and thus can be utilized. The B vitamins are distributed in most metabolizing tissues of plants and animals.

Water-soluble vitamins usually are excreted in the urine of humans. Thiamin, riboflavin, vitamin B6, vitamin C, pantothenic acid, and biotin appear in urine as free vitamins (rather than as coenzymes). However, little free niacin is excreted in the urine. Products (also called metabolites) that are formed during the metabolism of thiamin, niacin, and vitamin B6 also appear in the urine, as do urinary metabolites of biotin, riboflavin, and pantothenic acid. Excretion of these vitamins (or their metabolites) is low when intake is sufficient for proper body function. If intake begins to exceed minimal requirements, excess vitamins are stored in the tissues. Tissue storage capacity is limited, however, and, as the tissues become saturated, the rate of excretion increases sharply. Unlike the other water-soluble vitamins, however, vitamin B12 is excreted solely in the feces. Some folic acid and biotin also are normally excreted in this way. Although fecal excretion of water-soluble vitamins (other than vitamin B12, folic acid, and biotin) occurs, their source probably is the intestinal bacteria that synthesize the vitamins, rather than vitamins that have been eaten and utilized by the animal.

The water-soluble vitamins generally are not considered toxic if taken in excessive amounts. There is, however, one exception in humans: large amounts (50–100 mg; 1 mg = 0.001 gram) of niacin produce dilation of blood vessels. In larger amounts, the effects are more serious and may result in impaired liver function. Thiamin given to animals in amounts 100 times the requirement (i.e., about 100 mg) can cause death from respiratory failure. Therapeutic doses (100–500 mg) of thiamin have no known toxic effects in humans (except rare instances of anaphylactic shock in sensitive individuals). There is no known toxicity for any other B vitamins.

THE FAT-SOLUBLE VITAMINS

The four fat-soluble vitamin groups are A, D, E, and K. They are related structurally in that all have a basic five-carbon isoprene segment, shown here:

$$-\text{CH}=\text{CH}-\overset{\displaystyle\overset{\text{CH}_3}{|}}{\text{C}}=\text{CH}-$$

Each of the fat-soluble vitamin groups contains several related compounds that have biological activity. The potency of the active forms in each vitamin group varies, and not all of the active forms now known are available from dietary sources (i.e., some are produced synthetically). The characteristics of each fat-soluble vitamin group are discussed in the following sections.

CHEMICAL PROPERTIES

The chemical properties of fat-soluble vitamins determine their biological activities, functions, metabolism, and excretion. However, while the substances in each group of fat-soluble vitamins are related in structure, indicating that they share similar chemical properties, they do have important differences. These differences impart to the vitamins unique qualities, chemical and biological, that affect attributes ranging from the manner in which the vitamins are stored to the species in which they are active.

VITAMIN A GROUP

Ten carotenes, coloured molecules synthesized only in plants, show vitamin A activity. However, only the alpha- and beta-carotenes and cryptoxanthin are important to humans, and beta-carotene is the most active. Retinol (vitamin A alcohol) is considered the primary active form of the vitamin, although retinal, or vitamin A aldehyde, is the form involved in the visual process in the retina of the eye. A metabolite of retinol with high biological activity may be an even more direct active form than retinol. The ester form of retinol is the storage form of vitamin A. Presumably, it must be converted to retinol before it is utilized. Retinoic acid is a short-lived product of retinol. Only retinoic acid of the vitamin A group is not supplied by the diet.

VITAMIN D GROUP

Although about 10 compounds have vitamin D activity, the two most important ones are ergocalciferol (vitamin D2) and cholecalciferol (vitamin D3). Vitamin D3 represents the dietary source, while vitamin D2 occurs in yeasts and fungi. Both can be formed from their respective provitamins by

A woman indulges in a quick sunbathing session in a Paris, France, garden. The ultraviolet rays from sunlight convert provitamins in the skin to vitamin D_3. Franck Fife/AFP/Getty Images

ultraviolet irradiation. In humans and other animals the pro-vitamin (7-dehydrocholesterol), which is found in skin, can be converted by sunlight to vitamin D3 and thus is an important source of the vitamin. Both vitamin D2 and vitamin D3 can be utilized by rats and humans. However, chicks cannot use vitamin D2 effectively. The form of the vitamin probably active in humans is calcitriol.

VITAMIN E GROUP

The tocopherols are a closely related group of biologically active compounds that vary only in number and position

ADOLF WINDAUS

(b. Dec. 25, 1876, Berlin, Ger.—d. June 9, 1959, Göttingen, W.Ger.)

German organic chemist Adolf Windaus received the Nobel Prize for Chemistry in 1928 for research on substances, notably vitamin D, that play important biological roles.

After receiving his Ph.D. from the University of Freiburg (1899), Windaus held positions there and at Innsbruck, Austria, before being appointed head of the chemical institute at the University of Göttingen (1915–44). His studies of the chemical structure of cholesterol, begun in 1901, spanned some 30 years. This work was part of his study of the complex alcohols known as sterols.

Windaus discovered 7-dehydrocholesterol, which is the chemical precursor of vitamin D, and he showed that it is a steroid. He discovered that it is converted into the vitamin when one of its chemical bonds is broken by the action of sunlight. This explained why exposure to sunlight can prevent vitamin D deficiency (rickets) in humans. Windaus' research also helped establish the chemistry of the sex hormones and advanced the development of drugs used to treat heart ailments.

of methyl (-CH3) groups in the molecule. However, these structural differences influence the biological activity of the various molecules. The active tocopherols are named in order of their potency (i.e., alpha-tocopherol is the most active). Some metabolites of alpha-tocopherol (such as alpha-tocopherolquinone and alphatocopheronolactone) have activity in some mammals (e.g., rats, rabbits). However, these metabolites do not support all the functions attributed to vitamin E.

VITAMIN K GROUP

Vitamin K1 (20), or phylloquinone, is synthesized by plants. The members of the vitamin K2 (30), or menaquinone, series are of microbial origin. Vitamin K2 (20) is the important form in mammalian tissue. All other forms are converted to K2 (20) from vitamin K3 (menadione). Since vitamin K3 does not accumulate in tissue, it does not furnish any dietary vitamin K.

FUNCTIONS

The vitamin A group is essential for the maintenance of the linings of the body surfaces (e.g., skin, respiratory tract, cornea), for sperm formation, and for the proper functioning of the immune system. In the retina of the eye, retinal is combined with a protein called opsin. The complex molecules formed as a result of this combination and known as rhodopsin (or visual purple) are involved in dark vision. The vitamin D group is required for growth (especially bone growth or calcification). The vitamin E group also is necessary for normal animal growth—without vitamin E, animals are not fertile and develop abnormalities of the central nervous system, muscles, and organs (especially the liver). The vitamin K group is required for normal metabolism, including the conversion of food into cellular energy in certain biological membranes. Vitamin K also is necessary for the proper clotting of blood.

METABOLISM

The fat-soluble vitamins are transported primarily by lymph from the intestines to the circulating blood. Bile salts are required for efficient absorption of fat-soluble metabolites in the intestine. Anything that interferes with fat absorption, therefore, also inhibits absorption of the fat-soluble vitamins. Since a fatty acid (preferentially palmitic acid) is added to the retinol (vitamin A alcohol) molecule before it is transported by the lymph, this ester form predominates in the bloodstream during digestion. Vitamins D, E, and K do not require the addition of a fatty acid molecule for absorption. Small amounts of vitamin A (and possibly vitamin K) may be absorbed directly into the bloodstream. However, both vitamins A and D are bound to a protein during transport in the bloodstream.

Larger quantities of the fat-soluble vitamins than of water-soluble ones can be stored in the body. Vitamins A, D, and K are stored chiefly in the liver, with smaller amounts stored in other soft body tissues. Most of the stored vitamin E is found in body fat, although large amounts also occur in the uterus of females and testis of males. The various forms of vitamin E are stored in tissues in different amounts. For example, alpha-tocopherol is stored in higher concentrations than are the other forms. More vitamin A is stored than any other fat-soluble vitamin.

Excessive intakes of both vitamins A and D may produce toxicity (or hypervitaminosis A or D). Toxicity of these vitamins can easily occur, however, if pharmaceutical vitamin preparations are used in excess.

Toxic levels of vitamin A exceed the normal requirement by 100 times—i.e., about 150,000 µg each day for a period of several months. Toxicity in infants may occur with much smaller doses. Excessive doses of the natural vitamins K1 and K2 have no obvious effects except that resistance may develop to therapy with anticoagulant drugs. However, vitamin K3 is toxic to newborn infants if given in large doses. Vitamin E, even if given in large excess of the normal requirement, has no apparent obvious adverse effects.

Vitamin groups E and K belong to a class of organic compounds called quinones. These substances are changed to sugarlike substances known as alpha-lactones, which are excreted in the urine. Some vitamin K1 also is excreted in the bile and thus appears in the feces. Vitamin A is broken down and excreted in bile (and, therefore, feces) and urine. Vitamin D and its breakdown products are excreted only in the feces.

VITAMIN-LIKE SUBSTANCES

There are a number of organic compounds that, although related to the vitamins in activity, cannot be defined as true vitamins since normally they can be synthesized by humans in adequate amounts and therefore are not required in the diet. These substances usually are classified with the B vitamins, however, because of similarities in biological function or distribution in foods.

CHOLINE

Choline appears to be an essential nutrient for a number of animals and microorganisms that cannot synthesize adequate quantities to satisfy their requirements. Choline is a constituent of an important class of lipids called phospholipids, which form structural elements of cell membranes, and it is a component of the acetylcholine molecule, which is important in nerve function. Choline also serves as a source of methyl groups (-CH3 groups) that are required in various metabolic processes. The effects of a dietary deficiency of choline itself can be alleviated by other dietary compounds that can be changed into choline. Choline also functions in the transport of fats from the liver, and for this reason, it may be called a lipotropic factor. A deficiency of choline in the rat results in an accumulation of fat in the liver. Choline-deficiency symptoms vary among species, and it is not known if choline is an essential nutrient for humans since a dietary deficiency has not been demonstrated.

Myo-Inositol

The biological significance of myo-inositol has not yet been established with certainty. It is present in large amounts—principally as a constituent of phospholipids—in humans. Inositol is a carbohydrate that closely resembles glucose in structure. It can be converted to phytic acid, which is found in grains and forms an insoluble (and thus unabsorbable) calcium salt in the intestines of mammals. Inositol has not been established as an essential nutrient for humans. However, it is a required factor for the growth of some yeasts and fungi.

Para-Aminobenzoic Acid

Para-aminobenzoic acid (PABA) is required for the growth of several types of microorganisms, although a dietary requirement by vertebrates has not been shown.

The antimicrobial sulfa drugs (sulfanilamide and related compounds) inhibit the growth of bacteria by competing with PABA for a position in a coenzyme that is necessary for bacterial reproduction. Although a structural unit of folic acid, PABA is not considered a vitamin.

CARNITINE

Carnitine is essential for the growth of mealworms. The role of carnitine in all organisms is associated with the transfer of fatty acids from the bloodstream to active sites of fatty acid oxidation within muscle cells. Carnitine, therefore, regulates the rate of oxidation of these acids. This function may afford means by which a cell can rapidly shift its metabolic patterns (e.g., from fat synthesis to fat breakdown). Synthesis of carnitine occurs in insects and in higher animals, and therefore, it is not considered a true vitamin.

LIPOIC ACID AND BIOFLAVINOIDS

Lipoic acid has a coenzyme function similar to that of thiamin. Although it is apparently an essential nutrient for some microorganisms, no deficiency in mammals has been observed. Therefore, lipoic acid is not considered a true vitamin. The bioflavinoids once were thought to prevent scurvy and were designated as vitamin Pc, but additional evidence refuted this claim.

DETERMINATION OF VITAMIN SOURCES

A quantitative analysis of the vitamin content of foodstuffs is important in order to identify dietary sources of specific vitamins (and other nutrients as well). Three methods commonly used to determine vitamin content are described in the following sections.

PHYSICOCHEMICAL METHODS

The amount of vitamin in a foodstuff can be established by studying the physical or chemical characteristics of the vitamin, such as a chemically reactive group on the vitamin molecule, fluorescence, absorption of light at a wavelength characteristic of the vitamin, or radioisotope dilution techniques. These methods are accurate and can detect very small amounts of the vitamin. Biologically inactive derivatives of several vitamins have been found, however, and may interfere with such determinations. In addition, these procedures also may not distinguish between bound (i.e., unavailable) and available forms of a vitamin in a food.

MICROBIOLOGICAL ASSAY

Microbiological assay is applicable only to the B vitamins. The rate of growth of a species of microorganism that requires a vitamin is measured in growth media that contain various known quantities of a foodstuff preparation containing unknown amounts of the vitamin. The response (measured as rate of growth) to the unknown amounts of vitamin is compared with that obtained from a known quantity of the pure vitamin. Depending on the way in which the food sample was prepared, the procedure may indicate the availability of the vitamin in the food sample to the microorganism.

ANIMAL ASSAY

All of the vitamins, with the exception of vitamin B12, can be estimated by the animal-assay technique. One advantage of this method is that animals respond only to the biologically active forms of the vitamins. On the other hand, many other interfering and complicating factors may arise. Therefore, experiments must be rigidly standardized and controlled. Simultaneous estimates usually are made using a pure standard vitamin preparation as a reference and the unknown food whose vitamin content is being sought. Each test is repeated using two or more different amounts of both standard and unknown in the assays listed below.

In a growth assay, the rat, chick, dog (used specifically for niacin), and guinea pig (used specifically for vitamin C) usually are used. One criterion used in a vitamin assay is increase in body weight in response to different amounts of a specific vitamin in the diet. There are two types of growth assay. In a prophylactic growth assay, the increase in weight of young animals given different amounts of the vitamin is measured. In a curative growth assay, weight increase is measured in animals first deprived of a vitamin and then given various quantities of it. The curative growth assay tends to provide more consistent results than the prophylactic technique.

In a reaction time assay, an animal is first deprived of a vitamin until a specific deficiency symptom appears. Then the animal is given a known amount of a food extract containing the vitamin, and the deficiency symptom disappears within a day or two. The time required for the reappearance of the specific symptoms when the animal again is deprived of the vitamin provides a measure of the amount of vitamin given originally. The graded response assay, which may be prophylactic or curative, depends on a characteristic response that varies in degree with the vitamin dosage. An example of this technique is an assay for vitamin D in which the measured ash content of a leg bone of a rat or chick is used to reflect the amount of bone calcification that occurred as a result of administration of a specific amount of vitamin D. In an all-or-none assay, the degree of response cannot be measured. An arbitrary level is selected to separate positive responses from negative ones. The percent of positively reacting animals provides a measure of response. So, for example, vitamin E can be measured by obtaining the percent of fertility in successfully mated female rats.

DETERMINATION OF VITAMIN REQUIREMENTS

Biological studies may be performed to determine functions, effects of deprivation, and quantitative requirements of vitamins in various organisms. The development in an organism of a deficiency either by dietary deprivation of the vitamin or by administration of a specific antagonist or compound that prevents the normal function of the vitamin (antivitamin) often is the method used. The obvious effects (e.g., night blindness, anemia, dermatitis) of the deficiency are noted. Less obvious effects may be discovered after microscopic examination of tissue and bone structures.

Changes in concentrations of metabolites or in enzymatic activity in tissues, blood, or excretory products are examined by numerous biochemical techniques. The response of an animal to a specific vitamin of which it has been deprived usually confirms the deficiency symptoms for that vitamin. Effects of deprivation of a vitamin sometimes indicate its general physiological function, as well as its function at the cellular level. Biochemical function often is studied by observing the response of tissue enzymes (removed from a deficient host animal) after a purified vitamin preparation is added. The functions of most of the known vitamins have been reasonably well defined. However, the mechanism of action has not yet been established for some.

The procedure for determining the amount of a vitamin required by an organism is less difficult for microorganisms than for higher forms. In microorganisms, the aim is to establish the smallest amount of a vitamin that produces maximal rate of multiplication of the organisms when it is added to the culture medium. Among vertebrates, particularly humans, a number of procedures are used together to provide estimates of the vitamin requirement. These procedures include determinations of: the amount of a vitamin required to cure a deficiency that has been developed under controlled, standard conditions; the smallest amount required to prevent the appearance of clinical or biochemical symptoms of the deficiency; the amount required to saturate body tissues (i.e., to cause "spillover" of the vitamin in the urine; valid only with the water-soluble vitamins); the amount necessary to produce maximum blood levels of the vitamin plus some tissue storage (applicable only to the fat-soluble vitamins, particularly vitamin A); the amount required to produce maximum activity of an enzyme system if the vitamin has a coenzyme function; the actual rate of utilization, and hence the requirement, in healthy individuals (as indicated by measuring the excreted breakdown products of radioisotope-labeled vitamins).

The above procedures are practical only with small groups of animals or human subjects and thus are not entirely representative of larger populations of a particular species. A less precise, but more representative, method used among human populations involves comparing levels of dietary intake of a vitamin in a population that shows no deficiency symptoms with levels of intake of the vitamin in a population that reveals clinical or biochemical symptoms. The data for dietary intakes and incidence of deficiency symptoms are obtained by surveys of representative segments of a population.

CHAPTER 4

THE FOOD GROUPS AND REGULATION OF FOOD INTAKE

The foods that make up the traditional food groups are organized according to their nutritional characteristics. These divisions provide a useful classification system but also are important for helping people to strive toward and maintain a balanced diet. Individual diet is influenced directly by specific hungers, caloric needs, appetite, culture, and other factors, and thus some people may have difficulty consuming a balanced diet or may simply have different perceptions of food. In some places, healthy foods are inaccessible or expensive, and a lack of educational resources on proper nutrition may also result in an unbalanced diet.

THE FOOD GROUPS

The following nine food groups reflect foods with generally similar nutritional characteristics: (1) cereals, (2) starchy roots, (3) legumes, (4) vegetables and fruits, (5) sugars, preserves, and syrups, (6) meat, fish, and eggs, (7) milk and milk products, (8) fats and oils, and (9) beverages.

CEREALS

The cereals are all grasses that have been bred over millennia to bear large seeds (i.e., grain). The most important cereals for human consumption are rice, wheat, and corn (maize). Others include barley, oats, and millet. The

ELLEN SWALLOW RICHARDS

*(b. Dec. 3, 1842, Dunstable, Mass., U.S.—d.
March 30, 1911, Boston, Mass.)*

American chemist Ellen Swallow Richards was the founder of
the home economics movement in the United States. During
her career, she encouraged women to learn to cook with pure
foods as a way of ensuring good nutrition.

Ellen Swallow was educated mainly at home. She briefly
attended Westford Academy and also taught school for a
time. Swallow was trained as a chemist, earning an A.B. from
Vassar College in 1870 and, as the first woman admitted to the
Massachusetts Institute of Technology (MIT), a B.S. in 1873.
Vassar accepted her master's thesis the same year. She remained
at MIT for two more years of graduate studies, but she was not
awarded a Ph.D. In 1875 she married Robert Hallowell Richards,
an expert in mining and metallurgy at MIT.

In November 1876, at her urging, the Woman's Education
Association of Boston contributed funds for the opening of a
Woman's Laboratory at MIT. There, as assistant director under
Professor John M. Ordway, she began her work of encouraging
women to enter the sciences and of providing opportunities for
scientific training to capable and interested women. Courses
in basic and industrial chemistry, biology, and mineralogy were
taught, and through Ordway a certain amount of industrial and
government consulting work was obtained. Richards published
several books and pamphlets as a result of her work with the
Woman's Laboratory, including *The Chemistry of Cooking and
Cleaning* (1882; with Marion Talbot) and *Food Materials and Their
Adulterations* (1885).

From 1876 Richards was also head of the science section of
the Society to Encourage Studies at Home. In 1881, with Alice
Freeman Palmer and others, she was a founder of the Association
of Collegiate Alumnae (later the American Association of
University Women). The Woman's Laboratory closed in 1883,
by which time its students had been regularly admitted to MIT.

In 1884 Richards became assistant to Professor William R. Nichols in the institute's new laboratory of sanitation chemistry, and she held the post of instructor on the MIT faculty for the rest of her life. During 1887–89 she had charge of laboratory work for the Massachusetts State Board of Health's survey of inland waters.

In 1890, under Richards's guidance, the New England Kitchen was opened in Boston to offer to working-class families nutritious food, scientifically prepared at low cost, and at the same time to demonstrate the methods employed. From 1894 the Boston School Committee obtained school lunches from the New England Kitchen. Richards lobbied for the introduction of courses in domestic science into the public schools of Boston, and in 1897 she helped Mary M.K. Kehew organize a school of housekeeping in the Woman's Educational and Industrial Union that was later taken over by Simmons College. In 1899 Richards called a summer conference of workers in the fledgling field of domestic science at Lake Placid, New York. Under her chairmanship the series of such conferences held over the next several years established standards, course outlines, bibliographies, and women's club study guides for the field, for which the name "home economics" was adopted. In December 1908 the Lake Placid conferees formed the American Home Economics Association, of which Richards was elected first president. She held the post until her retirement in 1910, and in that time she established the association's *Journal of Home Economics*. In 1910 she was named to the council of the National Education Association with primary responsibility for overseeing the teaching of home economics in public schools. Among her other published works were *Home Sanitation: A Manual for Housekeepers* (1887), *Domestic Economy as a Factor in Public Education* (1889), *The Cost of Living* (1899), *Sanitation in Daily Life* (1907), and *Euthenics: The Science of Controllable Environment* (1912).

carbohydrate-rich cereals compare favourably with the protein-rich foods in energy value. In addition, the cost of production (per calorie) of cereals is less than that of almost all other foods and they can be stored dry for many years. Therefore, most of the world's diets are arranged to meet main calorie requirements from the cheaper carbohydrate foods. The major component of all grains is starch. Cereals contain little fat, with oats having an exceptional 9 percent. The amount of protein in cereals ranges from 6 to 16 percent but does not have as high a nutritive value as that of many animal foods because of the low lysine content.

Brown and white rice combining to form a modified yin yang symbol. Brown rice, which keeps the bran and germ intact, contains more B vitamins and fibre than polished white rice. © iStockphoto.com/Yong Hian Lim

Controversy exists as to the relative merits of white bread and bread made from whole wheat flour. White flour consists of about 72 percent of the grain but contains little of the germ (embryo) and of the outer coverings (bran). Since the B vitamins are concentrated mainly in the scutellum (covering of the germ), and to a lesser extent in the bran, the vitamin B content of white flour, unless artificially enriched, is less than that of brown flour. Dietary fibre is located mostly in the bran, so that white flour contains only about one-third of that in whole wheat flour.

White flour is compulsorily enriched with synthetic vitamins in a number of countries, including the United States and the United Kingdom, so that the vitamin content is similar to that of the darker flours. White flour, of course, still lacks fibre and any yet unidentified beneficial factors that may be present in the outer layers of the wheat.

The B vitamins are also lost when brown rice is polished to yield white rice. People living on white rice and little else are at risk for developing the disease beriberi, which is caused by a deficiency of thiamin (vitamin B1). Beriberi was formerly common in poor Asian communities in which a large proportion of the diet consisted of polished rice. The disease has almost completely disappeared from Asia with the advent of greater availability of other foods and, in some areas, fortification of the rice with thiamin.

Yellow corn differs from other cereals in that it contains carotenoids with vitamin A activity. (Another exception is a genetically modified so-called golden rice, which contains carotene, the precursor for vitamin A.) Corn is also lower in the amino acid tryptophan than other cereals. The niacin in corn is in a bound form that cannot be digested or absorbed by humans unless pretreated with lime (calcium hydroxide) or unless immature grains are eaten at the so-called milky stage (usually as sweet corn). Niacin is also formed in the body as a metabolite of the amino acid tryptophan, but this alternative source is not available when the tryptophan content is too low.

STARCHY ROOTS

Starchy roots consumed in large quantities include potatoes, sweet potatoes, yams, taro, and cassava. Their nutritive value in general resembles that of cereals. The potato, however, provides some protein (2 percent) and also contains vitamin C. The yellow-fleshed varieties of sweet potato contain the pigment beta-carotene, convertible in the body into vitamin A. Cassava is extremely low in protein, and most varieties contain cyanide-forming compounds that make them toxic unless processed correctly.

LEGUMES

Beans and peas are the seeds of leguminous crops that are able to utilize atmospheric nitrogen via parasitic microorganisms attached to their roots. Legumes contain at least 20 percent protein, and they are a good source of most of the B vitamins and of iron. Like cereals, most legumes are low in fat, though an important exception is the soybean (17 percent), a major commercial source of edible oil. Tofu, or bean curd, is made from soybeans and is an important source of protein in China, Japan, Korea, and Southeast Asia. Peanuts (groundnuts) are also the seeds of a leguminous plant, although they ripen underground. Much of the crop is processed for its oil.

VEGETABLES AND FRUITS

Vegetables and fruits have similar nutritive properties. Because 70 percent or more of their weight is water, they provide comparatively little energy or protein, but many contain vitamin C and carotene. However, cooked vegetables are an uncertain source of vitamin C, as this vitamin is easily destroyed by heat. The dark-green leafy vegetables are particularly good sources of vitamin A activity. Vegetables also provide calcium and iron but often in a form that is poorly absorbed. The more typical fruits, such as apples, oranges, and berries, are rich in sugar. Bananas are a good source of potassium. Vegetables and fruits also contain fibre, which adds bulk to the intestinal content and is useful in preventing constipation.

GETTING THE MOST FROM FRUIT

Not all fruits are created equal. To help people select the most nutritious fruits, Paul Lachance of Cook College at Rutgers University in New Jersey and Elizabeth Sloan of Applied Biometrics in Florida developed a rating system for 28 popular fresh fruits. They based their ratings on two parameters of nutrient density: (1) a "daily value" per 100 grams of nine nutritional factors (namely, protein, total vitamin A, thiamin [vitamin B1], riboflavin [vitamin B2], niacin, folic acid, vitamin C, calcium, and iron) and (2) calories per nutrient (the "cost" in calories to deliver 1 percent of each of the nine nutrients).

Kiwi was number one on their list, followed by papaya, cantaloupe, strawberries, mango, lemon, orange (Florida), red currants, mandarin orange, and avocado. As for those people whose personal favourites are low on the list, not to worry: Any fruit is better than no fruit at all.

Botanically, nuts are actually a kind of fruit, but they are quite different in character with their hard shell and high fat content. The coconut, for example, contains some 60 percent fat when dried. Olives are another fruit rich in fat and are traditionally grown for their oil.

SUGARS, PRESERVES, AND SYRUPS

One characteristic of diets of affluent societies is their high content of sugar. This is due in part to sugar added at the table or as an ingredient in candy, preserves, and sweetened colas or other beverages. The sugars, mostly sucrose and high-fructose corn syrup, together provide 12 percent of the average total calories in adults and a little more in children. There are also naturally occurring sugars in foods (lactose in milk and fructose, glucose, and sucrose in fruits and some vegetables). The intake of these in the United States is about 8 percent of total caloric intake in adults and much more in young children due to their greater intake of lactose in milk. Sugar, however, contains no protein, minerals, or vitamins and thus has been called the source of "empty calories."

Because sugar adsorbs water and prevents the growth of microorganisms, it is an excellent preservative. Making jam or marmalade is a way of preserving fruit, but most of the vitamin C is destroyed, and the products contain up to 70 percent sugar. Honey and natural syrups (e.g., maple syrup) are composed of more than 75 percent sugar.

MEAT, FISH, AND EGGS

Generally meats consist of about 20 percent protein, 20 percent fat, and 60 percent water. The amount of fat present in a particular portion of meat varies greatly, not only with the kind of meat but also with the quality. The "energy value" of meat varies in direct proportion with the fat content. Meat is valuable for its protein, which is of high biological value. Pork is an excellent source of thiamin. Meat is also a good source of niacin, vitamin B12, vitamin B6, and the mineral nutrients iron, zinc, phosphorus, potassium, and magnesium. Liver is the storage organ for, and is very rich in, vitamin A, riboflavin, and folic acid. In many cultures the organs (offal) of animals—including the kidneys, the heart, the tongue, and the liver—are considered delicacies. Liver is a particularly rich source of many vitamins.

The muscular tissue of fish consists of 13 to 20 percent protein, fat ranging from less than 1 to more than 20 percent, and 60 to 82 percent water that varies inversely with fat content. Many species of fish, such as cod and haddock, concentrate fat in the liver and as a result have extremely lean muscles. The tissues of other fish, such as salmon and herring, may contain 15 percent fat or more. However, fish oil, unlike the fat in land animals, is rich in essential long-chain fatty acids and is regarded as nutritionally advantageous. Large amounts of one of the major fatty acids, eicosapentaenoic acid, reduces the tendency to thrombosis.

The egg has a deservedly high reputation as a food. Its white contains protein, and its yolk is rich in both protein and vitamin A. An egg also provides calcium and iron. Egg yolk, however, has a high cholesterol content.

MILK AND MILK PRODUCTS

The milk of each species of animal is a complete food for its young. Moreover, one pint of cow's milk contributes about 90 percent of the calcium, 30 to 40 percent of the riboflavin, 25 to 30 percent of the protein, 10 to 20 percent of the calories and vitamins A and B, and up to 10 percent of the iron and vitamin D needed by a human adult.

Human breast milk is the perfect food for infants, provided it comes from a healthy, well-nourished mother and the infant is full-term. Breast milk contains important antibodies, white blood cells, and nutrients. In communities where hygiene is poor, breast-fed babies have fewer infections than formula-fed babies. In the past, infants who could not be breast-fed were given cow's milk that was partially "humanized" with the addition of water and a small amount of sugar or wheat flour. However, this was far from an ideal substitute for breast milk, being lower in iron and containing undenatured proteins that could produce allergic reactions with bleeding into the gut and, in some cases, eczema.

Lactose, the characteristic sugar of milk, is a disaccharide made of the monosaccharides glucose and galactose. Some adults can break down the lactose of large quantities of milk into galactose and glucose, but others have an inherited lactose intolerance as a result of the lactase enzyme no longer being secreted into the gut after the age of weaning. As a result, unabsorbed lactose is fermented by bacteria and produces bloating and gas. People who have little lactase in their bodies can still consume large amounts of milk if it has been allowed to go sour, if lactobacilli have split most of the lactose into lactic acid (as in yogurt), or if the lactose has been treated with commercially available lactase. People originating in northern Europe usually retain full intestinal lactase activity into adult life.

Most commercially available milk has been pasteurized with heat to kill bovine tuberculosis organisms and other possible pathogens. The most widely used method for pasteurizing milk is the high-temperature, short-time (HTST) sterilization treatment. If products are to be stored under refrigeration, or even at room temperature, for long periods of time, they may be processed by ultra-high-temperature (UHT) pasteurization. Another method of preserving milk without refrigeration involves the removal of water to form condensed milk, which can be exposed to air for several days without deterioration. Milk, either whole or defatted, can also be dried to a powder. In some countries, such as the United States, milk is homogenized so that fat particles are broken up and evenly distributed throughout the product.

Cow's milk is good food for human adults, but the cream (i.e., the fat) contains 52 percent saturated fatty acids as compared with only 3 percent polyunsaturated fat. This fat is either drunk with the milk or eaten in butter or cream. Because milk fat is regarded as undesirable by people who want to reduce their energy intake or cholesterol level, the dairy industry has developed low-fat cow's milk (with 2 percent fat instead of the almost 4 percent of whole milk), very low-fat skim milk, and skim milk with extra nonfat milk solids (lactose, protein, and calcium)

Swiss farmers collecting curd from a cauldron of milk to make Gruyere cheese. Fabrice Coffrini/AFP/Getty Images

that give more body to the milk. Buttermilk, originally the watery residue of butter making, is now made from either low-fat or skim milk that has been inoculated with nonpathogenic bacteria.

Cheese making is an ancient art formerly used on farms to convert surplus milk into a food that could be stored without refrigeration. Rennet, an enzyme found in a calf's stomach, is added to milk, causing the milk protein casein to coagulate into a semisolid substance called curd, thus trapping most of the fat. The remaining watery liquid (whey) is then drained, and the curd is salted, inoculated with nonpathogenic organisms, and allowed to dry and mature. Cheese is rich in protein and calcium and is a good source of vitamin A and riboflavin. Most cheeses, however, contain about 25 to 30 percent fat (constituting about 70 percent of the calories of the cheese), which is mostly saturated, and they are usually high in sodium.

FATS AND OILS

The animal fats used by humans are butter, suet (beef fat), lard (pork fat), and fish oils. Important vegetable oils include olive oil, peanut (groundnut) oil, coconut oil, cottonseed oil, sunflower seed oil, soybean oil, safflower oil, rapeseed oil, sesame (gingelly) oil, mustard oil, red palm oil, and corn oil. Fats and oils provide more calories per gram than any other food, but they contain no protein and few micronutrients. Only butter and the previously mentioned fish-liver oils contain any vitamin A or D, though red palm oil does contain carotene, which is converted to vitamin A in the body. Vitamins A and D are added to margarines. All natural fats and oils contain variable amounts of vitamin E, the fat-soluble vitamin antioxidant.

The predominant substances in fats and oils are triglycerides, chemical compounds containing any three fatty acids combined with a molecule of glycerol. A small group of fatty acids is essential in the diet. They occur in body structures, especially the different membranes inside and around cells, and cannot be synthesized in the body from other fats. Linoleic acid is the most important of these fatty acids because it is convertible to other essential fatty acids. Linoleic acid has two double bonds and is a polyunsaturated fatty acid. As well as being an essential fatty acid, it tends to lower the cholesterol level in the blood. Linoleic acid occurs in moderate to high proportions in many of the seed oils (e.g., corn, sunflower, cottonseed, and safflower oils). Some margarines (polyunsaturated margarines) use a blend of oils selected to provide a moderately high linoleic acid content.

BEVERAGES

Although most adults drink about one to two quarts (one to two litres) of water a day, much of this is in the form of liquids such as coffee, tea, fruit juices, and soft drinks. In general, these are appreciated more for their taste or for their effects than for their nutritive value. Fruit juices are, of course, useful for their vitamin C content and are good sources of potassium. Coffee and tea by themselves are of no nutritive value, except that coffee contains some niacin and tea contains fluoride and manganese. These beverages also contain natural caffeine, which has a stimulating effect. Caffeine is added to colas, and so-called diet soft drinks contain small quantities of artificial sweeteners in place of sugars so that their overall calorie value is reduced.

Since ethyl alcohol (ethanol) has an energy value of 7 kilocalories per gram, very significant amounts of energy can be obtained from alcoholic drinks. Beer contains 2 to 6 percent alcohol, wines 10 to 13 percent, and most spirits up to 40 percent. Fermented drinks also include significant amounts of residual sugars, and champagne and dessert wines may have sugar added to them. With one or two exceptions, alcoholic beverages contain no nutrients and are only a source of "empty calories." The only vitamin present in significant amounts in beer is riboflavin. Wines are devoid of vitamins but sometimes contain large amounts of iron, probably acquired from iron vessels used in their preparation. Heavy alcohol consumption is known to lead to a greater risk of malnutrition, in part because it can damage the absorptive power of the gut and also because heavy drinkers commonly neglect to follow a normal pattern of meals. On the other hand, evidence from a number of studies shows that persons consuming one to two drinks per day are healthier than are those who abstain from drinking alcohol. This might be due in part to substances in red wine, such as flavonoids and tannins, which may protect against heart disease.

REGULATION OF FOOD INTAKE

From a basic physiological perspective, the regulation of food intake is governed by the opposing states of hunger and satiety, each of which relies on communication between the stomach, where physical sensations arise, and the brain, where the sensations are interpreted. Thus, whereas an empty stomach experiencing contractions (hunger pangs) sends electrical impulses, or signals, to the brain that communicate hunger, a full stomach sends signals communicating satiety. A variety of factors, however, are capable of confusing this basic mechanism. For example, the smell, taste, or appearance of food or one's desire to eat (appetite) can influence food intake. Likewise, fear or anxiety and learned behaviours, such as food preferences, can play a significant role in determining the amount and types of foods an individual consumes. Hence, psychological factors can have a significant influence on food intake, to the point of overriding basic physiological sensations. Extremes of this influence are reflected in cases of excess weight gain (obesity) and weight loss (anorexia nervosa).

SPECIFIC HUNGERS

Lack of any nutrient with a specific anabolic function, such as vitamins or minerals, must be redressed by increased uptake of the particular substance. Little is known thus far of the specific hunger mechanisms that ensure increased uptake, but good evidence exists that a nutrient deficiency causes a specific rise in responsiveness to food containing the substance needed.

In the case of thiamine (vitamin B1), a learning process is involved. A person deficient in this vitamin may try eating various kinds of food and then concentrate on those foods that remove the deficiency. Specific appetite for salt in a sodium deficient subject, on the other hand, appears to rest on a genetically determined increase in reaction to the taste of sodium chloride and does not require any learning.

CALORIC REGULATION

Lack of fuel in the body can be corrected by intake of any of a variety of possible substances that provide energy. Most natural food contains a mixture of such substances. Energy deficiencies can be alleviated by increased responsiveness to food in general. Ingested food (i.e., calories) passes from the mouth to the digestive tract, to the bloodstream. If not needed at once for catabolic processes, the digested food passes to storage sites, of which the fat tissues are the most important. These regions are continuously monitored.

A considerable amount is known about the monitoring roles of the organs for taste, smell, and touch in the mouth region. In addition, distension receptors in the digestive tract monitor the volume there, and chemoreceptors monitor the nature of the contents. Information concerning the availability of glucose (the most commonly utilized sugar) and possibly other fuels in the blood is recorded by cells located probably both in the brain itself and elsewhere (e.g., in the liver). Finally, there is some evidence suggesting that the contents of fat tissues are also monitored. All food that passes through the body contributes to each of these four messages in succession, until it is eventually catabolized.

A teenage boy eating salty potato chips. A craving for salt may indicate a sodium deficiency. Pascal Broze/Getty Images

The signals converge on the brain mechanisms for the feeding motivation over nervous and, possibly, humoural (chemical) pathways. Here they have effects of two kinds: (1) if signals from the four regions report increased fuel contents, the feeding motivation is lowered (satiety is raised), and (2) if taste (and perhaps other, e.g., visual) receptors are stimulated by palatable food the feeding motivation is increased. Intake stops when accumulation of signals of the first kind, overriding those of the second kind, causes hunger to drop below a critical level. Feeding is resumed when hunger surpasses this level as a result of fuel depletion by catabolism and emptying of the digestive tract by digestion and absorption. Once started, intake is enhanced by the positive effects of the food stimulus. The net result of this interplay of positive and negative feedbacks from food responses is that caloric intake, observed over a sufficiently long period (at least several days), is equal to energy output over that period, so that body fuel content (body weight in fully grown individuals) remains constant.

The brain mechanisms involved in the motivation to eat consist of a complex network, not fully understood, encompassing, among other areas of the brain, the limbic system (the marginal zone of the forebrain) and the hypothalamus. The lateral hypothalamus ("hunger centre") facilitates feeding responses. Electrical or chemical stimulation of this area elicits voracious feeding in satiated subjects, and its destruction causes more or less prolonged noneating (aphagia). If the subject is kept alive by artificial feeding, however, other brain areas may take over and reinstate more or less normal feeding. In contrast, the ventromedial (lower central) nucleus of the hypothalamus appears to be a clearinghouse for satiety signals. Subjects with lesions in this area stop feeding only at an abnormally high level of energy content (obesity) and grossly overeat (hyperphagia) until this level is reached.

APPETITE

Appetite is the desire to eat. It is influenced by a number of hormones and neurotransmitters (substances released by neurons to stimulate neighbouring neurons), which have been classified as appetite stimulants or appetite suppressants. Many of these substances are involved in mediating metabolic processes. For example, the gastrointestinal substance known as ghrelin, which regulates fat storage and metabolism, stimulates appetite. Likewise, agouti-related protein and neuropeptide Y, substances produced in the brain, act as appetite stimulants. In animals and humans appetite suppressants include melanocyte-stimulating hormone, insulin, and leptin, a protein hormone secreted by adipose cells that acts on the hypothalamus in the brain.

Appetite is often associated with the desire to eat particular foods based on their smell, flavour, appearance, and appeal. This is a primary factor separating appetite from the primary motive of hunger. In addition, a person may be totally filled with food from a meal and still have an "appetite" for dessert. Furthermore, appetite may be increased or diminished depending on pleasant or unpleasant experiences associated with certain foods.

SATIETY

Satiety is the desire to limit further food intake, as after completing a satisfying meal. The hypothalamus regulates the amount of food desired. Several hypotheses have been developed to explain the mechanism of regulation. One hypothesis is that eating increases body temperature, and as the temperature in the hypothalamus rises, the process of feeding decreases. A second hypothesis suggests that as food enters the gastrointestinal tract, peptides (small proteins) that act on the brain to produce satiety are released from the gut. Other hypotheses focus on the role of fat or glucose in mediating hypothalamic regulation.

Satiety is reached long before food is digested or absorbed. In humans a number of factors may be involved in limiting food consumption. The feeling of fullness caused by distention of the stomach can stop further eating. A large quantity of sugar in the bloodstream or a large amount of stored fat tissue may inhibit ingestion. Emotional or psychological factors also can cause or delay satiety. A person who is upset may be totally satisfied by only a few bites of food. People on diets can limit their food intake by refraining from eating before reaching satiety, in which case the body may crave more nourishment, but the desire to eat more can be overruled.

DIETING

Dieting is the regulation of one's food intake for the purpose of improving one's physical condition, especially for the purpose of reducing excess body fat. Dieting plans are based on the reduction of any of the macronutrients (fats, carbohydrates, and proteins) that constitute the major portions of food that a person eats (other than water) and that are necessary sources of energy. Energy deficits of 500–1,000 calories per day produce rather rapid initial weight loss owing to the early loss of body water, especially if carbohydrates are restricted. But, after the initial effects of dehydration, all the dieting plans produce a rate of fat loss that can only be proportional to the caloric deficit.

CHAPTER 5

NUTRITIONAL IRREGULARITIES

Nutritional irregularities consist of deficits or toxicities. Insufficient intake of foods or nutrients such as vitamins are a primary cause of nutritional deficiencies. However, deficiencies may also be produced by an inability to absorb or metabolize nutrients. Toxicities are produced by overconsumption of foods or certain nutrients. With few exceptions, these conditions apply to virtually all types of macronutrients and micronutrients, including water. Because of the extensive array of vitamin deficiencies and toxicities, vitamin irregularities are discussed separately in this book.

MALNUTRITION

Malnutrition is a physical condition resulting either from a faulty or inadequate diet (i.e., a diet that does not supply normal quantities of all nutrients) or from a physical inability to absorb or metabolize nutrients, owing to disease. Malnutrition may be the result of several conditions. First, sufficient and proper food may not be available because of inadequate agricultural processes, imperfect distribution of food, or certain social problems, such as poverty or alcoholism. In these instances, the cause of malnutrition is most often found to be a diet quantitatively inadequate in calories or protein.

Malnutrition may also result when certain foods containing one or more of the essential vitamins or minerals are

An Ethiopian mother and her children showing signs of malnourishment. Longstanding drought has made growing food very difficult in the country, leading to widespread malnutrition. Alain Buu/Gamma-Rapho/GettyImages

not included in the diet. This commonly leads to specific nutritional-deficiency diseases. Poor eating habits and food preferences may lead to malnutrition through the habitual consumption of certain foods to the exclusion of others or of large quantities of nonnutritious foods. In certain parts of Africa, for example, the practice of weaning breast-fed infants to a diet consisting chiefly of one kind of starchy food, such as cassava, may lead to protein deficiency. In parts of East Asia, a restricted selection of foods and a preference for white polished rice as a dietary staple has led to the prevalence of a deficiency of thiamin (vitamin B1), which is found mainly in the germ and bran of grain. Multiple deficiencies are more likely to occur than single deficiencies, though the manifestations of one type usually predominate.

Malnutrition can also arise from acquired or inherited metabolic defects, notably those involving the digestive tract, liver, kidney, and red blood cells. These defects cause malnutrition by preventing the proper digestion, absorption, and metabolism of foodstuffs by organs and tissues.

PROTEIN-ENERGY MALNUTRITION

Chronic undernutrition manifests primarily as protein-energy malnutrition (PEM), which is the most common form of malnutrition worldwide. Also known as protein-calorie malnutrition, PEM is a continuum in which people—all too often children—consume too little protein, energy, or both. At one end of the continuum is kwashiorkor, characterized by a severe protein deficiency, and at the other is marasmus, an absolute food deprivation with grossly inadequate amounts of both energy and protein.

Treatment of PEM has three components. (1) Life-threatening conditions—such as fluid and electrolyte imbalances and infections—must be resolved. (2) Nutritional status should be restored as quickly and safely as possible (rapid weight gain can occur in a starving child within one or two weeks). (3) The focus of treatment then shifts to ensuring nutritional rehabilitation for the long term. The speed and ultimate success of recovery depend upon the severity of malnutrition, the timeliness of treatment, and the adequacy of ongoing support. Particularly during the first year of life, starvation may result in reduced brain growth and intellectual functioning that cannot be fully restored.

Protein deficiencies can also occur in hospitalized patients receiving intravenous glucose for an extended time, as when recovering from surgery, or in those with illnesses causing loss of appetite or malabsorption of nutrients. Persons with eating disorders, cancer, AIDS, and other illnesses where appetite fails or absorption of nutrients is hampered may lose muscle and organ tissue as well as fat stores.

KWASHIORKOR SYNDROME

Kwashiorkor syndrome is a condition caused by severe protein deficiency. Kwashiorkor is most often encountered in developing countries in which the diet is high in starch and low in proteins. It is common in young children weaned to a diet consisting chiefly of cereal grains, cassava, plantain, and sweet potato or similar starchy foods.

The condition in children was first described in 1932. The term *kwashiorkor* means "deposed child" ("deposed" from the mother's breast by a newborn sibling) in one African dialect and "red boy" in another dialect. The latter term comes from the reddish orange discoloration of the hair that is characteristic of the disease. Other symptoms include dry skin and skin rash, potbelly and edema, weakness, nervous irritability, anemia, digestive disturbances such as diarrhea, and fatty infiltration of the liver. Weight loss in kwashiorkor may be disguised by edema, enlarged fatty liver, and intestinal parasites. Moreover, there may be little wasting of muscle and body fat. However, children with this disease grow poorly, and they are highly susceptible to infectious diseases.

In addition to protein-deficient diet, other causes of kwashiorkor include poor intestinal absorption, chronic alcoholism, kidney disease, and infection, burns, or other trauma resulting in the abnormal loss of body protein. The consumption of dried milk-based formula has proved effective in treating kwashiorkor. As long-term preventive measures, such international groups as the World Health

Organization and the Food and Agriculture Organization of the United Nations have actively encouraged the successful development of high-protein plant mixtures based on local food preferences and availability. Protein malnutrition in early life may lead to an adult predisposition to certain diseases such as cirrhosis of the liver and may cause stunted mental development.

MARASMUS

Marasmus is a form of protein-energy malnutrition occurring chiefly among very young children in developing countries, particularly under famine conditions, in which a mother's milk supply is greatly reduced. Marasmus results from the inadequate intake of both protein and calories (in contrast, persons with kwashiorkor do not obtain enough protein but still consume a moderate number of calories). Marasmus is characterized by growth retardation (in weight more than in height) and progressive wasting of subcutaneous fat and muscle. The affected child may become acutely emaciated and fail to grow. Other symptoms may include diarrhea; dehydration; behavioral changes; dry, loose skin; and dry, brittle hair. Severe, prolonged marasmus may result in permanent intellectual disability.

The nutritional deficiencies in marasmus can be caused by early weaning to a bottled formula prepared with unsafe water and diluted because of poverty. Poor hygiene and continued depletion lead to a vicious cycle of gastroenteritis and deterioration of the lining of the gastrointestinal tract, which interferes with absorption of nutrients from the little food available and further reduces resistance to infection. Marasmus can be treated with a high-calorie, protein-rich diet. If untreated, it may result in death due to starvation or heart failure.

JOHN BOYD ORR

(b. Sept. 23, 1880, Kilmaurs, Ayrshire, Scot.—d. June 25, 1971, Edzell, Angus)

Scottish scientist John Boyd Orr was an authority on nutrition and the winner of the 1949 Nobel Prize for Peace.

Boyd Orr received a scholarship to attend the University of Glasgow, where he enrolled in a teacher-training program and was a student of theology. As part of his scholarship, he was required to teach for a period. After receiving a master's degree in 1902, he was given a teaching post at a school in the city's slums, where he witnessed firsthand the ill effects of poverty on children. Within days he resigned from the post and returned home, being reassigned to teach at Kyleshill School in Saltcoats, North Ayrshire.

Upon completing his teaching obligations, Boyd Orr turned to medicine and the study of nutrition. He returned to the University of Glasgow, earning a bachelor's degree in science in 1910 and a medical degree in 1914. During his graduate studies, he conducted research into protein metabolism and studied the effects of water intake on nitrogen metabolism and blood pressure. Also in 1914 he became director of the Institute of Animal Nutrition (now Rowett Research Institute) at the University of Aberdeen. However, the institute was not built when Boyd Orr arrived in Aberdeen. He was given £5,000 to begin building the institute and was required to raise funds for its completion. Following a stint as a medical officer in the British army and navy during World War I, Boyd Orr returned to Aberdeen and managed to raise enough money to finish the institute's construction.

In the early 1920s Boyd Orr investigated metabolism in ruminants and the role of minerals in the health of farm animals. In 1925 he visited Africa, where he learned about the diets of local farm animals and indigenous peoples. He made subsequent trips to the Middle East, India, and elsewhere, exploring various indigenous diets and local farming and animal husbandry practices. He later investigated the nutritional value of cow's milk for humans, discovering that the addition of milk to the diets of British children led to increases in the children's weight and height. In 1929, following his research on animal nutrition, he founded the Imperial Bureau of Animal Nutrition at Aberdeen.

Boyd Orr first gained fame with the publication of *Food, Health and Income* (1936), a report of a dietary survey by income groups made during 1935 that showed that the cost of a diet fulfilling basic nutritional requirements was beyond the means of half the British population and that 10 percent of the population was undernourished. This and other reports conducted by the Rowett Research Institute formed the basis of the British food-rationing system during World War II.

During the war, Boyd Orr was a member of the cabinet's scientific committee on food policy and held the chair of agriculture at the University of Aberdeen. In 1945 he became rector of the University of Glasgow, a member of Parliament for the Scottish universities, and director general of the United Nations Food and Agriculture Organization (FAO), serving in the latter until 1948. While head of the FAO, Boyd Orr developed a proposal for a World Food Board that would facilitate the transfer of surplus food from food-exporting countries to food-deprived countries upon request by the latter. Once hunger and poverty were eliminated, the food loans would be repaid, without interest. The proposal, considered extraordinarily ambitious, was defeated at a meeting in Copenhagen in 1946. Despite this setback, Boyd Orr was awarded the Nobel Prize for his efforts to eliminate world hunger.

CARBOHYDRATE DEFICIENCY

Under most circumstances, there is no absolute dietary requirement for carbohydrates—simple sugars, complex carbohydrates such as starches, and the indigestible plant carbohydrates known as dietary fibre. Certain cells, such as brain cells, require the simple carbohydrate glucose as fuel. If dietary carbohydrate is insufficient, glucose synthesis depends on the breakdown of amino acids derived from body protein and dietary protein and the compound glycerol, which is derived from fat. Long-term carbohydrate inadequacy results in increased production of organic compounds called ketones (a condition known as ketosis), which imparts a distinctive sweet odour to the breath. Ketosis and other untoward effects of a very-low-carbohydrate diet can be prevented by the daily consumption of 50 to 100 grams of carbohydrate. However, obtaining at least half of the daily energy intake from carbohydrates is recommended and is typical of human diets, corresponding to at least 250 grams of carbohydrate (1,000 calories in a 2,000-calorie diet). A varied diet containing fruits, vegetables, legumes, and whole-grain cereals, which are all abundant in carbohydrates, also provides a desirable intake of dietary fibre.

DEFICIENCIES IN ESSENTIAL FATTY ACIDS

There is also a minimum requirement for fat—not for total fat, but only for the fatty acids linoleic acid (a so-called omega-6 fatty acid) and alpha-linolenic acid (an omega-3 fatty acid). Deficiencies of these two fatty acids have been seen in hospitalized patients fed exclusively with intravenous fluids containing no fat for weeks, patients with medical conditions affecting fat absorption, infants given formulas low in fat, and young children fed nonfat milk or low-fat diets. Symptoms of deficiency include dry skin, hair loss, and impaired wound healing. Essential fatty acid requirements—a few grams a day—can be met by consuming approximately a tablespoon of polyunsaturated plant oils daily. Fatty fish also provides a rich source of omega-3 fatty acids. Even individuals following a low-fat diet generally consume sufficient fat to meet requirements.

MINERAL DEFICIENCIES

Reductions in the levels of essential minerals can have serious impacts on human health, causing, for example, impaired brain function, abnormal bone growth, or altered nerve activity. Mineral deficiencies affect people in developed and less-developed countries alike. However, because large numbers of people may not have access to essential minerals in less-developed countries, the conditions tend to be more widespread in those places. Some of the most common mineral deficiencies include iron deficiency, iodine deficiency, and calcium deficiency.

IRON DEFICIENCY

Iron deficiency is the most common of all nutritional deficiencies, with much of the world's population being deficient in the mineral to some degree. The main function of iron is in the formation of hemoglobin, the red pigment of the blood that carries oxygen from the lungs to other tissues. Since each millilitre of blood contains 0.5 mg of iron (as a component of hemoglobin), bleeding can drain the body's iron reserves. When iron stores are depleted, a condition arises known as microcytic hypochromic anemia, characterized by small red blood cells that contain less hemoglobin than normal.

Symptoms of severe iron deficiency anemia include fatigue, weakness, apathy, pale skin, difficulty breathing on exertion, and low resistance to cold temperatures. During childhood, iron deficiency can affect behaviour and learning ability as well as growth and development. Severe

A Palestinian girl suffering from chronic anemia waits to be treated in the Gaza Strip. Iron deficiency is most common in infants and young children. Paula Bronstein/Getty Images

anemia increases the risk of pregnancy complications and maternal death.

Iron deficiency anemia is most common during late infancy and early childhood, when iron stores present from birth are exhausted and milk, which is poor in iron, is a primary food; during the adolescent growth spurt; and in women during the childbearing years because of blood loss during menstruation and the additional iron needs of pregnancy. Therefore, young children and premenopausal women are the most vulnerable.

Intestinal blood loss and subsequent iron deficiency anemia in adults may also stem from ulcers, hemorrhoids, tumours, or chronic use of certain drugs such as aspirin. In developing countries, blood loss due to hookworm and other infections, coupled with inadequate dietary iron intake, exacerbates iron deficiency in both children and adults.

IODINE DEFICIENCY

Iodine deficiency is a condition in which iodine is insufficient or is not utilized properly. Iodine is an element that directly affects thyroid gland secretions, which themselves to a great extent control heart action, nerve response to stimuli, rate of body growth, and metabolism.

Iodine is essential for normal thyroid hormone production and can be obtained only from the diet. The recommended daily iodine intake is 150 µg daily for adults, 220 µg daily for pregnant women, and 290 µg daily for lactating women. Worldwide, iodine deficiency is the most common cause of thyroid disease. Iodine deficiency is most prevalent in persons living in mountainous areas, where the soil and therefore the food and water contain very small amounts of iodine. In contrast, the condition is least common in persons living in coastal areas, where the soil often contains large amounts of iodine and where iodine-rich seafood is likely to be consumed. It can be prevented by an adequate dietary intake of iodine, which is most often achieved by the addition of iodine to salt.

When iodine intake is low, thyroid hormone production decreases. This results in an increase in thyrotropin secretion by the pituitary gland. Increased thyrotropin secretion stimulates the thyroid to take up more of the iodine that is available, using it to produce thyroid hormone. In addition, thyrotropin stimulates the growth of thyroid cells. Thus, although the compensatory increase in secretion of the hormone acts to minimize the decrease in thyroid hormone production, it also causes enlargement of the thyroid gland, resulting in goiter. Many people with iodine deficiency have only very mild hypothyroidism, which is a decrease in thyroid hormone production that is characterized by symptoms of dry skin, hair loss, a puffy face, weakness, weight increase, fatigue, and mental sluggishness. In very young infants, even a minor degree of hypothyroidism is sufficient to cause intellectual disability. Severe iodine deficiency, particularly during gestation and in the first months following birth, can result in cretinism. Children and adolescents with iodine deficiency typically have diffuse goiter, which will decrease in size if iodine intake is increased. However, in adults the goiter

An African woman awaits treatment for the goitre, or large lump, in her neck. A goitre occurs when the thyroid becomes enlarged, possibly due to a lack of sufficient iodine in a person's diet. Per-Anders Pettersson/Getty Images

becomes nodular and does not regress when iodine intake is increased.

Prevention of iodine deficiency is most simply accomplished by eating seafood regularly or by using iodized table salt. To overcome natural iodine deficits, government health officials in many countries worldwide have made dietary iodine additives mandatory.

ZINC DEFICIENCY

A constituent of numerous enzymes, zinc plays a structural role in proteins and regulates gene expression. Zinc deficiency in humans was first reported in the 1960s in Egypt and Iran, where children and adolescent boys with stunted growth and undeveloped genitalia responded to treatment with zinc. Deficiency of the mineral was attributed to the regional diet, which was low in meat and high in legumes, unleavened breads, and whole-grain foods that contain fibre, phytic acid, and other factors that inhibit zinc absorption. Also contributing to zinc deficiency was the practice of clay eating, which interferes with the absorption of zinc, iron, and other minerals. Severe zinc deficiency has also been described in patients fed intravenous solutions inadequate in zinc and in the inherited zinc-responsive syndrome known as acrodermatitis enteropathica.

Symptoms of zinc deficiency may include skin lesions, diarrhea, increased susceptibility to infections, night blindness, reduced taste and smell acuity, poor appetite, hair loss, slow wound healing, low sperm count, and impotence. Zinc is highest in protein-rich foods, especially red meat and shellfish, and zinc status may be low in protein-energy malnutrition. Even in developed countries, young children, pregnant women, the elderly, strict vegetarians, people with alcoholism, and those with malabsorption syndromes are vulnerable to zinc deficiency.

CALCIUM DEFICIENCY

Calcium is the mineral that is most likely to be deficient in the average diet. It is the chief supportive element in bones and teeth. Calcium salts make up about 70 percent of bone by weight and give that substance its strength and rigidity. About 99 percent of the calcium in the human body is held in the bones and teeth. The remaining 1 percent circulates in the bloodstream, where it performs a variety of important functions. It helps to contract muscles and to regulate the contractions of the heart. It plays a role in the transmission of nerve impulses and in the clotting of blood. Calcium is involved in the stimulation of contractions of the uterus during childbirth and in the production of milk. It also regulates the secretion of various hormones and aids in the functioning of various enzymes within the body.

Ingested calcium is absorbed in the small intestine and passes from there into the bloodstream, most of it ultimately reaching the bones and teeth. The most efficient absorption of calcium is dependent on the presence in the body of vitamin D, which is a key ingredient in various hormones that enable calcium to pass from the digestive system into the blood, bones, and teeth. Similarly, there are optimal ratios of phosphorus to the amount of calcium consumed that permit calcium to be more completely utilized. Hormonal secretions of the parathyroid and thyroid glands (parathyroid hormone and calcitonin, respectively) also help maintain a calcium equilibrium in the blood. These regulatory mechanisms help to prevent a deficiency in calcium from developing in the bloodstream. When such a deficiency does develop, parathyroid hormone and vitamin D act to transfer calcium from the bones in order to maintain the mineral's all-important presence in the bloodstream. The result of a mild insufficiency of calcium over the long term may be a factor in osteoporosis, a disease characterized by thinning of the bones. Faulty metabolism of calcium during childhood may result in rickets. Recent research points to calcium deficiency as being a possible cause of hypertension (high blood pressure) and of colorectal cancer.

Severe calcium deficiency, or hypocalcemia, which is defined as a reduction of calcium levels in the bloodstream below a certain normal range, has its own clinical manifestations. The main syndrome is tetany, which involves sensations of numbness and tingling around the mouth and fingertips and painful aches and spasms of the muscles. These symptoms respond to treatment with calcium. A clinically detectable deficiency of calcium is a relatively rare finding and is almost always caused by a deficiency of either parathyroid hormone or vitamin D in the body (i.e., the two chief regulators of calcium metabolism).

Calcium is plentiful in nature. Food sources high in calcium include milk, cheese, yogurt, and other dairy products; leafy green vegetables such as broccoli, turnips, and collard greens; and seafood such as salmon and sardines.

FLUORIDE DEFICIENCY

Fluoride deficiency is a condition in which fluoride is insufficient or is not utilized properly. Fluoride is a mineral stored in teeth and bones that strengthens them by aiding in the retention of calcium. Studies have determined that the enamel of sound teeth contains more fluoride than is found in the teeth of persons prone to dental caries, and the incidence of dental caries is reduced in areas where natural fluoridation of water is moderate. For these reasons, fluoride is added to water supplies in some areas to help reduce tooth decay, although such actions have in some cases provoked controversy. Excess amounts of fluoride may cause tooth mottling, which presents no problem other than appearance. Massive doses of fluoride can be lethal, and fluorides are used as the toxic ingredient of many insect poisons.

SODIUM DEFICIENCY

Sodium is usually provided in ample amounts by food, even without added table salt (sodium chloride). Furthermore, the body's sodium-conservation mechanisms are highly developed, and thus sodium deficiency is rare, even for those on low-sodium diets. Sodium depletion may occur during prolonged heavy sweating, vomiting, or diarrhea or in the case of kidney disease. Symptoms of hyponatremia, or low blood sodium, include muscle cramps, nausea, dizziness, weakness, and eventually shock and coma. After prolonged high-intensity exertion in the heat, sodium balance can be restored by drinking beverages containing sodium and glucose (sports drinks) and by eating salted food. Drinking 4 cups (one litre) of water containing one-third teaspoon (two millilitres) of table salt also should suffice.

Chloride is lost from the body under conditions that parallel those of sodium loss. Severe chloride depletion results in a condition known as metabolic alkalosis (excess alkalinity in body fluids).

CHLORINE DEFICIENCY

Chlorine is a component of all body secretions and excretions resulting from processes of building and breaking down body tissues. Levels of chlorine closely parallel levels of sodium intake and output, since a primary source of both is sodium chloride, or common table salt. Chlorine is stored to a limited extent in the skin, subcutaneous tissues, and skeleton and constitutes two-thirds of the negatively charged ions (anions) in the blood. Chlorides (chlorine compounds) play an essential role in the electrical neutrality and pressure of extracellular fluids and in the acid-base balance of the body. Gastric secretion is composed of chlorides in the form of hydrochloric acid and salts.

Chlorine is readily absorbed during digestion, and similarly its rate of excretion through sweat, kidney excretion, and intestinal expulsion is high. The body's supplies of chlorine are rapidly depleted during hot weather, when excessive perspiration reduces the fluid content of the body. Also, stored chlorides may become dangerously low in periods of severe vomiting and diarrhea and in diseases that produce severe alkalosis, an accumulation of base or loss of acid in the body.

Treatment of chlorine deficiency is directed toward the underlying cause. The best source of chlorine is ordinary table salt, but chlorides are also naturally contained in meat, milk, and eggs. Almost all canned foods have salt added during the canning process.

POTASSIUM DEFICIENCY

Potassium is an essential constituent of cellular fluids, and its storage in body cells is dependent on maintenance of a proper ratio with calcium and sodium. Potassium is important for normal muscle and nerve responsiveness, heart rhythm, and, in particular, intracellular fluid pressure and balance. Approximately 8 percent of the potassium that the body takes in through food consumption is retained, while the rest is readily excreted.

Potassium deficiency is also called hypokalemia. Deficiency problems are not usually a result of poor nutrition but may arise in poor societies where malnutrition is common. Rapid excretion of potassium in severe diarrhea, diabetes, and prolonged administration of cortisone medications are among the causes of nondietary deficiencies. A lack of potassium is known to exaggerate the effects of sodium in decreases and increases of normal metabolic activity. In one form of potassium depletion, which is the loss of adequate potassium in the tissues, including the blood, the potassium has not left the body but has shifted into the body cells from the fluid surrounding them.

Symptoms of potassium deficiency include weakness, loss of appetite, muscle cramps, and confusion. Severe hypokalemia (low blood potassium) may result in cardiac arrhythmias. Potassium-rich foods, such as bananas or oranges, can help replace losses of the mineral, as can potassium chloride supplements, which should be taken only under medical supervision.

MINERAL TOXICITY

A desirable dietary intake of the minerals generally falls in a fairly narrow range. Because of interactions, a high intake of one mineral may adversely affect the absorption or utilization of another. Excessive intake from food alone is unlikely, but consumption of fortified foods or supplements increases the chance of toxicity. Furthermore, environmental or occupational exposure to potentially toxic levels of minerals presents additional risks for certain populations.

Widespread calcium supplementation, primarily by children who do not drink milk and by women hoping to prevent osteoporosis, has raised concerns about possible adverse consequences of high calcium intake. A major concern has been kidney stones (nephrolithiasis), the majority of which are composed of a calcium oxalate compound. For years, a low-calcium diet was recommended for people at risk of developing kidney stones, despite disappointing effectiveness and a fair amount of research challenging the approach. However, there eventually emerged strong evidence that a diet relatively low in sodium and animal protein with normal amounts of calcium (1,200 mg per day) is much more effective in preventing recurrent stone formation than was the traditional low-calcium diet. In fact, dietary calcium may be protective against kidney stones because it helps bind oxalate in the intestine. Constipation is a common side effect of high calcium intake, but daily consumption of up to 2,500 mg is considered safe for adults and for children at least one year old.

The use of magnesium salts in medications, such as antacids and laxatives, may result in diarrhea, nausea, and abdominal cramps. Impaired kidney function renders an individual more susceptible to magnesium toxicity. Excess magnesium intake is unlikely from foods alone.

High-dose iron supplements, commonly used to treat iron deficiency anemia, may cause constipation and other gastrointestinal effects. A daily iron intake of up to 45 mg presents a low risk of gastrointestinal distress. Acute toxicity and death from ingestion of iron supplements is a major poisoning hazard for young children. In people with the genetic disorder hereditary hemochromatosis, a disease characterized by the overabsorption of iron, or in those who have repeated blood transfusions, iron can build up to dangerous levels, leading to severe organ damage, particularly of the liver and heart. It is considered prudent for men and postmenopausal women to avoid iron supplements and high iron intakes from fortified foods. Toxicity from dietary iron has been reported in South Africa and Zimbabwe in people consuming a traditional beer with an extremely high iron content.

Excess zinc has been reported to cause gastrointestinal symptoms such as nausea and vomiting. Chronic intake of large amounts of zinc may interfere with the body's utilization of copper, impair immune response, and reduce the level of high-density lipoprotein (HDL) cholesterol (the so-called good cholesterol). A safe intake of 40 mg of zinc daily is unlikely to be exceeded by food alone, although it may be exceeded by zinc lozenges or supplements, which are widely used despite a lack of data about their safety or efficacy.

Selenium is toxic in large amounts. Selenosis (chronic selenium toxicity) results in symptoms such as gastrointestinal and nervous system disturbances, brittleness and loss of hair and nails, a garliclike odour to the breath, and skin rash. There also have been reports of acute toxicity and death from ingestion of gram quantities of the mineral. Excess selenium can be harmful whether ingested as selenomethionine, the main form found in food, or in the inorganic forms usually found in supplements. A daily intake of up to 400 µg from all sources most likely poses no risk of selenium toxicity.

Impaired thyroid gland function, goiter, and other adverse effects may result from high intakes of iodine from food, iodized salt, or pharmaceutical preparations intended to prevent or treat iodine deficiency or other disorders. Although most people are unlikely to exceed safe levels, individuals with certain conditions, such as autoimmune thyroid disease, are particularly sensitive to excess iodine intake.

While the teeth are developing and before they erupt, excess fluoride ingestion can cause mottled tooth enamel, although this is only a cosmetic effect. In adults, excess fluoride intake is associated with effects ranging from increased bone mass to joint pain and stiffness and, in extreme cases, crippling skeletal fluorosis. Even in communities where water supplies naturally provide fluoride levels several times higher than recommended, skeletal fluorosis is extremely rare.

High intakes of phosphorus (as phosphate) may affect calcium metabolism adversely and interfere with the absorption of trace elements such as iron, copper, and zinc. However, even with the consumption of phosphate additives in a variety of foods and in cola beverages, exceeding safe levels is unlikely. Manganese toxicity, with central nervous system damage and symptoms similar to Parkinson's disease, is a well-known occupational hazard of inhaling manganese dust, but again, it is not likely to come from the diet. Similarly, copper toxicity is unlikely to result from excessive dietary intake, except in individuals with hereditary or acquired disorders of copper metabolism.

DEHYDRATION

Dehydration may be caused by restricted water intake, excessive water loss, or both. The most common cause of dehydration is failure to drink liquids. The deprivation of water is far more serious than the deprivation of food. The loss of water from the body is almost invariably associated with some loss of salt (sodium chloride) as well. The treatment of any form of dehydration, therefore, requires not only the replacement of the water lost from the body but also the restoration of the normal concentration of salt within the body fluid.

The average person loses approximately 2.5 percent of total body water per day (about 1.25 quarts [1,200 millilitres]) in urine, in expired air, by insensible perspiration, and from the gastrointestinal tract. If, in addition to this loss, the loss through perspiration is greatly increased—as is demonstrated in the case of the shipwrecked sailor in tropical seas or the traveler lost in the desert—dehydration may result in shock and death within only a few hours. When swallowing is difficult in extremely ill persons, or when people cannot respond to a sense of thirst because of age or illness or dulling of consciousness, the failure to compensate for the daily loss of body water will result rapidly in dehydration and its consequences. Large volumes of water also may be lost from the body by vomiting or diarrhea.

The symptoms of dehydration depend in part on the cause and in part on whether there is associated salt deprivation as well. When loss of water is disproportionately greater than loss of electrolytes (salt), the osmotic pressure of the extracellular fluids becomes higher than in the cells. Since water passes from a region of lower to a region of higher osmotic pressure, water flows out of the cells into the extracellular fluid, tending to lower its osmotic pressure and increase its volume toward normal. As a result of the flow of water out of the cells, they become dehydrated. This results in the thirst that always accompanies "pure" water depletion.

In those diseases in which there is loss of salt in excess of water loss, the decreased concentration of sodium in the extracellular fluid and in the blood serum results in decreased osmotic pressure, and water therefore enters the cells to equalize the osmotic pressure. Thus there is extracellular dehydration and intercellular hydration—and no thirst.

Water deprivation produces distinctive symptoms in humans. Weight loss, amounting to two to three pounds per day, occurs. Thirst is the most prominent symptom, with the dryness of mouth, decreased production of saliva, and impaired swallowing that accompany it. It is probable that thirst is the result of this subsequent intracellular dehydration and increased intracellular osmotic pressure. Experimentally, thirst can be produced when the cells have lost about 1 percent of their intracellular water.

As dehydration progresses, the tissues tend to shrink, the skin becomes dry and wrinkled, and the eyes become sunken and the eyeballs soft. Fever develops, possibly from mild to marked, as dehydration progresses. Dehydration itself probably affects the temperature regulatory centres in the brain. As dehydration and salt loss progress, however, the plasma volume and heart output decrease, with a consequent decrease in blood supply to the skin. Sweating decreases and may stop completely, and the main avenue for heat loss is closed. The body temperature may then rise precipitously.

There are marked changes in the volume of the extracellular and intracellular fluids, but the blood plasma volume changes the last and the least. The plasma volume is maintained more or less constant at the expense of the tissue fluids. If, however, the plasma volume does fall, the output of the heart also falls, and the pulse rate climbs, all of which indicates a dangerous physical state.

The renal (kidney) changes that occur in humans during prolonged water depletion similarly tend to maintain a normal balance. If water deprivation continues and the plasma volume falls, however, the output of urine will be drastically reduced. As long as urine output of more than 1 ounce (30 millilitres) per hour is maintained, the kidney can excrete nitrogenous and nonnitrogenous solids with maximum efficiency. Once the urine flow is decreased below this level, the kidney is unable to function efficiently, the substances are retained in the body, and their concentration in the blood rises.

The final result of prolonged dehydration is now apparent. The normal distribution of salt and water in the body is destroyed, the plasma volume decreases, and the blood viscosity increases. As a result of these changes renal function is impaired, the urinary output falls, and waste products accumulate. Far more life-threatening, however, is decreased loss of moisture from the skin, with the subsequent rise in temperature, and the fall in cardiac output with the attendant irreversible shock.

Once renal failure occurs, about 8 percent of the total body water has been lost (4.25 quarts [about 4 litres]). When 5.25 to 10.5 quarts (about 5 to 10 litres) of body water have been lost, a person is acutely and severely ill, with contracted plasma volume, increased concentration and viscosity of the blood, renal failure and excessive urea in the blood, and falling blood pressure. In a previously healthy adult, death follows the loss of 12.5 to 15.8 quarts (about 12 to 15 litres) of body water. In the very young, the very old, or the debilitated, death occurs at a lower level of dehydration.

The treatment of any form of dehydration depends not only on restoring the depleted water but also on reestablishing normal levels of body electrolytes and limiting the production of nitrogenous waste products. Before any of these therapeutic measures can be applied, however, the initiating cause must be removed. The sailor or the desert traveler must be rescued, the vomiting infant must be cured, or the underlying disease must be treated. Then, after accurate biochemical determinations of the levels of various electrolytes and other blood components have been made and the plasma volume has been measured, the physician may give measured quantities of the appropriate mixtures of salt and water. Given the right amounts of salt and water, the human body will gradually restore the normal relationships between the cells, the extracellular fluid, and the plasma volume. That done, the complicated functions of the kidney will clear the circulating blood of the retained waste products, and the body will have restored its own normal balance.

CHAPTER 6

VITAMIN DEFICIENCY AND TOXICITY

Although deficiency diseases have been described in laboratory animals and humans deprived of single vitamins, in human experience multiple deficiencies are usually present simultaneously. In some cases—such as with the eight B-complex vitamins, which function in coordination in numerous enzyme systems and metabolic pathways—a deficiency of one vitamin may affect the functioning of others. In addition to deficiencies, some persons are affected by vitamin toxicities, which can cause serious health complications.

VITAMIN A DEFICIENCY

Deficiency of vitamin A results in various disorders that most commonly involve the eye and the epithelial tissues. In humans, one of the earliest signs of vitamin A deficiency is night blindness (nyctalopia), the visual failure to adapt promptly from light to darkness and to see in the dark. This aspect of vision is normally dependent on rhodopsin, which maintains its photosensitivity only in the presence of vitamin A.

If the deficiency is severe and persists, especially in malnourished infants and children, a condition known as xerophthalmia may develop. In xerophthalmia, the eyes are sensitive to light, the secretion of lubricating tears is stopped, and the eyelids become swollen and sticky with

A child in Mumbai, India, having her eyes examined. Eye diseases occur more frequently in countries such as India and Bangladesh, where dairy products rich in vitamin A are not readily available. © AP Images

pus. The mucous surfaces of the eye may become eroded in spots, allowing infection to set in, thus leading to ulceration and other destructive changes of the cornea (the transparent outer covering of the eye) and other eye structures. This condition will eventually result in blindness. Except in the later stages, when cellular damage in the cornea and associated deeper structures is too extensive, xerophthalmia can be effectively treated with vitamin A. It is usually most effective when supported by a well-balanced diet rich in protein. Although xerophthalmia is seldom encountered in countries where dairy products are readily available, it is common among poor children in Indonesia, Bangladesh, India, and the Philippines, and occurs in some parts of Africa. The global incidence has been estimated at some 500,000 new cases per year, half of which lead to blindness. In order to prevent xeropthalmia, infants in some countries are given a single large dose of vitamin A at six months of age, followed by another dose four to six months later.

Early signs of vitamin A deficiency may also be reflected in changes in the mucous membranes of the mouth, throat, and respiratory and genito-urinary passages. These lining membranes become atrophied and dry and lose their cilia, the tiny hairlike projections that normally help in clearing away foreign particles. The defective mucous surfaces have weakened resistance to bacterial invasion, and their susceptibility to various infections increases. If insufficient intake of vitamin A is prolonged, the skin may become dry and rough, with the appearance of plugs of horny material about the hair follicles (follicular hyperkeratosis).

VITAMIN D DEFICIENCY

Lack of vitamin D in children causes rickets, a disease characterized by inadequate mineralization of bone, growth retardation, and skeletal deformities such as bowed legs. The adult form of rickets, known as osteomalacia, results in weak muscles as well as weak bones. Inadequate vitamin D may also contribute to the thinning of bones seen in osteoporosis. Individuals with limited sun exposure (including women who completely cover their bodies for religious reasons), elderly or homebound persons, and those with dark skin, particularly those who live in northern latitudes, are at risk of vitamin D deficiency. Vitamin D is found in very few foods naturally. Thus fortification of milk and other foods (e.g., margarine, cereals, and breads) with the vitamin has helped protect those populations in which sun exposure is inadequate. Supplemental vitamin D also may help protect against bone fractures in the elderly, who make and activate vitamin D less efficiently even if exposed to sunlight.

RICKETS

Following its production in the skin or absorption in the gastrointestinal tract, vitamin D is transported through the blood to the liver, where it is converted to calcidiol (25-hydroxyvitamin D). Calcidiol is then transported through the blood to the kidneys, where it is metabolized to calcitriol (1,25-dihydroxyvitamin D), the most active form of vitamin D. Calcitriol stimulates the small intestine, bone, and kidney to absorb calcium, as well as the minerals phosphate and magnesium. In bone, the absorption process leads to the deposition of the inorganic salt calcium phosphate, which is responsible for bone rigidity.

In the absence of calcitriol, the calcium absorption process does not proceed normally. Low serum calcium concentrations prompt the secretion of a substance known as parathormone from the parathyroid glands. Parathormone liberates calcium from bone in order to restore serum calcium concentrations. Hence, although the production of osteoid, the protein matrix on which calcium is deposited, is normal or increased in vitamin D deficiency, the matrix is poorly calcified. This results in soft bones, the literal meaning of the term *osteomalacia*

While rickets is said to arise generally from a lack of vitamin D in the body, specific causes have been described. For example, vitamin D deficiency can result from a lack of the vitamin in the diet, insufficient conversion in the skin by ultraviolet light, inefficient dietary absorption, or the abnormal conversion of vitamin D to its metabolites. Contributing factors to the development of rickets in children include having been breast-fed exclusively for a prolonged period of time (human breast milk contains low amounts of vitamin D), living in temperate regions where sunlight exposure is limited in winter, and having dark-pigmented skin. Certain underlying conditions, such as liver, kidney, or gastrointestinal disease, can interfere with the normal metabolism or absorption of vitamin D. In chronic kidney disease, for example, the conversion of calcidiol to calcitriol is decreased or absent, resulting in an inability to absorb calcium.

In other instances, rickets and rickets-type disorders may be caused by inherited defects in genes whose products are involved in vitamin D or phosphate metabolism. In hereditary hypophosphatemic rickets, for example, an increased rate of phosphate clearance from the body by the renal tubules of the kidneys results in loss of bone mineral and, in severe cases, in rickets-type deformities and dwarfism. The disease, which is rare and is most commonly inherited as an X-linked dominant disorder (one copy of the mutated gene on the X chromosome is sufficient to produce the disease), tends to start in early childhood.

Another inherited form of rickets is vitamin D-dependent rickets type I (VDDRI), in which a defect in the enzyme that converts calcidiol to calcitriol produces vitamin D deficiency and causes the loss of calcium from bone. Vitamin D-dependent rickets type II (VDDRII) involves loss-of-function mutations in a gene for the vitamin D receptor, with the result that tissues are unable to absorb calcitriol. VDDRII is associated with rickets, hypocalcemia (decreased serum calcium), and in some cases alopecia (baldness). Both VDDRI and VDDRII are autosomal recessive (two copies of the mutated gene, one from each parent, are required to cause disease) and manifest in infancy or early childhood.

A variety of similar syndromes exist. For example, de Toni–Fanconi syndrome is characterized by rickets deformities and renal tubule defects. In addition, tumours that produce substances capable of inhibiting the reabsorption of phosphate by the kidneys (oncogenic osteomalacia) may lead to rickets-type deformities. Tumours that cause hypophosphatemia (decreased serum phosphate) are often hard to locate because they are small and occur in fibrous or mesenchymal tissue, including bone.

Softened bones are readily curved, and their growth is stunted. In rickets there also is an overgrowth of cartilage, resulting in the enlargement of the ends of long bones and in the junction of the ribs with the rib cage in the chest (rachitic rosary). Common early symptoms of rickets include restlessness; profuse sweating; lack of muscle tone in the limbs and abdomen; softening of the bones of the skull; delay in learning to sit, crawl, and walk; and delay in the eruption of the teeth. Tetany (spasms of the hands and feet as well as cramps and twitching of the muscles) may also occur. Unless treatment is begun early, rickets may produce conditions such as bowlegs, knock-knees, a bulging forehead, and short stature. A narrowed chest and pelvis may be responsible later in life for increased susceptibility to lung diseases and difficulties in childbearing, respectively.

Rickets is diagnosed through an assessment of family medical history, X-rays, and blood and urine tests. A combination of X-rays, which reveal bone deformities characteristic of rickets, and knowledge of calcium, phosphate, calcidiol, and calcitriol levels typically leads to a definitive diagnosis.

Rickets is usually effectively treated with large supplemental doses of vitamin D concentrates (often in the form of calcitriol), with exposure to sunlight, and with a well-balanced diet. Vitamin D supplementation, usually in fortified milk, has been important in preventing the incidence of rickets in northern and temperate climates. Inherited forms of rickets often are treated with massive doses of vitamin D and supplementary phosphate and calcium.

The first treatment found to be effective for rickets was cod liver oil. Cod liver oil and exposure to sunlight were recognized as preventive and curative therapies for nutritional rickets in humans in the 18th and 19th centuries, respectively; however, these treatments were not generally accepted until the early 20th century. The existence of a vitamin able to mimic the effects of cod liver oil was indicated in experimental animals in 1918. In 1924 it was demonstrated that the curative effects of ultraviolet light resulted from the formation of vitamin D by such irradiation. Up until that time, vitamin D deficiency was a worldwide problem, particularly in the temperate zones. With the isolation of vitamin D2 (ergocalciferol, the form of vitamin D found in plants and fungi) in 1930–31 in England and Germany and of 7-dehydrocholesterol (the precursor of vitamin D) from hog skin in 1937 in Germany, the fortification of foods with the vitamin became possible.

As a result of therapeutic developments in the 20th century, the prevalence of rickets decreased, particularly in developed countries such as the United States, the United Kingdom, and Australia, where it eventually became rare. Today the distribution and prevalence of rickets are aligned primarily with risk factors. Hence, it is most prevalent in peoples who are dark-skinned and in developing countries where access to vitamin D-fortified foods is lacking. Africa, the Middle East, and parts of Asia rank among the world's most heavily affected regions.

OSTEOMALACIA

Osteomalacia is a condition in which the bones of an adult progressively soften because of inadequate mineralization of the bone. Osteomalacia may occur after several pregnancies or in old age, resulting in increased susceptibility to fractures. Symptoms include bone pain, weakness, numbness of the extremities, and spasms of the hands or feet.

Depletion of the bone minerals may be caused by lack of dietary vitamin D (or its precursor, ergosterol), inadequate exposure to sunlight (necessary for the formation of vitamin D in the body), impaired function of one of the organs involved in the absorption or metabolism of the bone minerals or vitamin D, frequent ingestion of mineral oil (in which vitamin D dissolves but is not absorbed from the intestines), or abnormalities in the bone mineralization process.

Individuals with osteomalacia frequently have multiple nutrient deficiencies. Treatment includes a well-balanced diet high in protein and calcium and supplemented in moderation with vitamin D concentrates or fish-liver oils.

VITAMIN E DEFICIENCY

Vitamin E deficiency is rare in humans, although it may develop in premature infants and in people with impaired fat absorption or metabolism. In the former, fragility of red blood cells (hemolysis) is seen, and in the latter, where deficiency is more prolonged, neuromuscular dysfunction involving the spinal cord and retina may result in loss of reflexes, impaired balance and coordination, muscle weakness, and visual disturbances. No specific metabolic function has been established for vitamin E. However, it is an important part of the antioxidant system that inhibits lipid peroxidation—in other words, it protects cells and their membranes against the damaging effects of free radicals (reactive oxygen and nitrogen species) that are produced metabolically or enter the body from the environment. The requirement for vitamin E is increased with increasing consumption of polyunsaturated fatty acids. People who smoke or are subjected to air pollution may also need more of the vitamin to protect against oxidative damage to the lungs.

VITAMIN K DEFICIENCY

Vitamin K is necessary for the formation of prothrombin and other blood-clotting factors in the liver, and it also plays a role in bone metabolism. A form of the vitamin is produced by bacteria in the colon and can be utilized to some degree. Vitamin K deficiency causes impaired clotting of the blood and internal bleeding, even without injury.

A disease that is usually associated with a lack of vitamin K is hypoprothrombinemia, which is characterized by a deficiency of the blood-clotting substance prothrombin, resulting in a tendency to prolonged bleeding. In adults the condition occurs most commonly in cases of obstructive jaundice, in which the flow of bile to the bowel is interrupted—bile being necessary for the intestinal absorption of vitamin K. Hypoprothrombinemia can also result from a general impairment in liver and intestinal-cell function or can follow exposure to dicumarol and related therapeutic anticoagulants.

Vitamin K deficiency in adults may also be associated with syndromes involving poor fat absorption or may occur in individuals with liver disease. Bleeding due to vitamin K deficiency may be seen in patients whose gut bacteria have been killed by antibiotics. Due to poor transport of vitamin K across the placenta, newborn infants in developed countries are routinely given the vitamin intramuscularly or orally within six hours of birth to protect against a condition known as hemorrhagic disease of the newborn.

DEFICIENCIES IN B VITAMINS

Deficiencies in the B vitamins can occur for a variety of reasons, including malnutrition, imbalanced diet, drug use, and exposure to substances that prevent uptake or interfere with B-vitamin metabolism. Symptoms of B-vitamin deficiency range from fatigue, indigestion, and restlessness to abnormalities in heart rhythm, tingling sensations in the extremities, and depression. The specific set of symptoms produced depends on which B vitamin is lacking since symptoms often are associated with the functions a vitamin normally carries out. In general, vitamin B deficiencies can be overcome through removal of the cause or through dietary supplementation.

THIAMIN DEFICIENCY

Prolonged deficiency of thiamin (vitamin B1) results in beriberi, a disease that has been endemic in populations where white rice has been the staple. Thiamin deficiency can also occur in populations eating large quantities of raw fish harbouring intestinal microbes that contain the enzyme thiaminase. In the developed world, thiamin deficiency is linked primarily to chronic alcoholism with poor diet, manifesting as Wernicke's encephalopathy, Korsakoff's syndrome (Korsakoff's psychosis, or Korsakoff's disease), or the combined Wernicke-Korsakoff syndrome.

Wernicke's encephalopathy is a neurological disorder that results from a deficiency of thiamine and is characterized by damage to nerves in both the central and peripheral nervous system. In some cases, it progresses to Korsakoff's syndrome or occurs with Korsakoff's

BERIBERI

Beriberi is a nutritional disorder caused by a deficiency of thiamin and characterized by impairment of the nerves and heart. General symptoms include loss of appetite and overall lassitude, digestive irregularities, and a feeling of numbness and weakness in the limbs and extremities. (The term *beriberi* is derived from the Sinhalese word meaning "extreme weakness.") In the form known as dry beriberi, there is a gradual degeneration of the long nerves, first of the legs and then of the arms, with associated atrophy of muscle and loss of reflexes. In wet beriberi, a more acute form, there is edema (overabundance of fluid in the tissues) resulting largely from cardiac failure and poor circulation. In infants breast-fed by mothers who are deficient in thiamin, beriberi may lead to rapidly progressive heart failure.

The cardiac symptoms, in both infants and adults, generally respond promptly and dramatically to the administration of thiamin. When neurological involvement is present, the response to thiamin is much more gradual. In severe cases, the structural lesions of the nerve cells may be irreversible.

Thiamin normally plays an essential role as a coenzyme in the metabolism of carbohydrates. In its absence, pyruvic acid and lactic acid (products of carbohydrate digestion) accumulate in the tissues, where they are believed to be responsible for most of the neurological and cardiac manifestations.

Thiamin occurs widely in food but may be lost in the course of processing, particularly in the milling of grains. In East Asian countries, where polished white rice is a dietary staple, beriberi has been a long-standing problem. The history of the recognition, the cause, and the cure of beriberi is dramatic and is well documented in medical literature. In the 1880s the Japanese navy reported that beriberi had been eradicated among its sailors as a result of adding extra meat, fish, and vegetables to their regular diet. Before that time, almost half of the sailors were likely to develop beriberi, and many died of it.

The prevention of beriberi is accomplished by eating a well-balanced diet, since thiamin is present in most raw and untreated foods. The incidence of beriberi in Asia has markedly decreased because an improved standard of living has allowed a more varied diet and partly because of the gradual popular acceptance of partially dehusked, parboiled, and enriched rice—forms that contain higher concentrations of thiamin. In Western countries, thiamin deficiency is encountered almost solely in cases of chronic alcoholism.

syndrome to produce Wernicke-Korsakoff syndrome, a condition marked by rapid eye movements, loss of muscle coordination, mental confusion, and memory loss. Korsakoff's syndrome itself is a neurological disorder characterized by severe amnesia (memory loss) that is often caused by thiamin deficiency in the brain. Affected individuals typically are unable to remember events in the recent or even the immediate past, and some can store information for only a few seconds before they forget it. The patient may also have forgotten a much longer time period, extending back for as many as 20 years. Another feature that is sometimes present is confabulation, in which the patient recounts detailed and convincing memories of events that never happened. Korsakoff's syndrome sometimes occurs as a transient manifestation of some other brain disorder.

RIBOFLAVIN DEFICIENCY

Riboflavin (vitamin B2) deficiency, known as ariboflavinosis, is unlikely without the simultaneous deficiency of other nutrients. After several months of riboflavin deprivation, symptoms include cracks in the skin at the corners of the mouth, fissures of the lips, and an inflamed, magenta-coloured tongue. Because riboflavin is readily destroyed by ultraviolet light, jaundiced infants who are treated with light therapy are administered the vitamin. Milk, milk products, and cereals, major sources of riboflavin in the diet, are packaged to prevent exposure to light.

NIACIN DEFICIENCY AND PELLAGRA

Pellagra is a nutritional disorder caused by a dietary deficiency of niacin (also called nicotinic acid) or a failure of the body to absorb this vitamin or the amino acid tryptophan, which is converted to niacin in the body. Pellagra is characterized by skin lesions and by gastrointestinal and neurological disturbances. The so-called classical three Ds of pellagra are dermatitis, diarrhea, and dementia.

Skin lesions result from an abnormal sensitization of the skin to sunlight and tend to occur symmetrically on the exposed surfaces of the arms, legs, and neck. They may look at first like a severe sunburn, later becoming reddish brown, rough, and scaly. Gastrointestinal symptoms usually consist of diarrhea, with an accompanying inflammation of the mouth and the tongue and fissuring and dry scaling of the lips and corners of the mouth. Neurological signs appear later in most cases, when the skin and alimentary manifestations are prominent. The dementia, or mental aberrations, may include general nervousness, confusion, depression, apathy, and delirium.

In humans, pellagra is seldom a deficiency of niacin alone. Response to niacin therapy tends to be partial, whereas the therapeutic administration of a well-balanced, high-protein diet and multivitamins commonly brings swift recovery. Mild or suspected instances of niacin deficiency can be effectively treated with a well-balanced diet alone.

Research by Joseph Goldberger of the United States Public Health Service and others showed that pellagra was the result of a nutritional deficiency. In 1937 it was shown that dogs with a disorder similar to pellagra known as black tongue could be cured by the administration of niacin. Pellagra is now seldom encountered in countries in which the population generally eats a well-balanced diet, but it still occurs in most countries in which people live on a diet that consists predominantly of corn (maize), which is low in tryptophan, and contains little or no protein-rich food. Such foods as milk and eggs, although low in niacin, will protect the body from pellagra because their proteins contain sufficient tryptophan for the synthesis of niacin. Pellagra can also be a side effect of chronic alcoholism. Symptoms closely resembling those of pellagra are seen in Hartnup disease.

VITAMIN B6 DEFICIENCY

Vitamin B6 (pyridoxine and related compounds) is essential in protein metabolism, the synthesis of neurotransmitters, and other critical functions in the body. Deficiency symptoms include dermatitis, microcytic hypochromic anemia (small, pale red blood cells), impaired immune function, depression, confusion, and convulsions. Although full-blown vitamin B6 deficiency is rare, marginal inadequacy is more widespread, especially among the elderly, who may have a reduced ability to absorb the vitamin. People with alcoholism, especially those with the liver diseases cirrhosis and hepatitis, are at risk of deficiency. A number of drugs, including the tuberculosis drug isoniazid, interfere with vitamin B6 metabolism.

FOLIC ACID DEFICIENCY AND ANEMIA

Vitamin B12 and folic acid (folate) are two B vitamins with many closely related functions, notably participation in

DNA synthesis. As a result, people with deficiencies of either vitamin show many of the same symptoms, such as weakness and fatigue due to megaloblastic anemia, a condition in which red blood cells, lacking sufficient DNA for cell division, are large and immature.

Folic acid deficiency anemia results from a deficient intake of folic acid, which is needed for the formation of heme, the pigmented, iron-containing portion of the hemoglobin in red blood cells (erythrocytes). A deficient intake of folic acid impairs the maturation of young red blood cells, which results in anemia. The disease also is characterized by leukopenia (a deficiency of white blood cells, or leukocytes), by thrombocytopenia (a deficiency of platelets), by ineffective blood formation in the bone marrow, and by progressive gastrointestinal symptoms, such as sore tongue, fissures at the corners of the mouth, diarrhea, inflammation of the pharynx or esophagus, and ulceration of the stomach and intestine. Folic acid deficiency develops over a period of several months and may result from a diet that is low or lacking in foods containing folic acid. The deficiency may also be brought on by poor absorption of folic acid in the intestine due to celiac disease or anticonvulsant drug therapy or by faulty metabolism of the vitamin in the liver due to cirrhosis.

Folic acid deficiency can also occur in pregnant women. Inadequate intake in early pregnancy may cause neural tube defects in the fetus. Thus, women capable of becoming pregnant are advised to take 400 µg of folic acid daily from supplements, fortified foods (such as fortified cereals), or both—in addition to consuming foods rich in folic acid such as fresh fruits and vegetables (especially leafy greens) and legumes.

Other conditions in folic acid deficiency that may occur include severe hemolytic anemia (dissolution of red blood cells by hemolysin) and exposure to the cancer drug

Drinking orange juice is recommended for pregnant women because the liquid is rich in folic acid, which is crucial for the fetus's development. © iStockphoto.com/Mark Bowden methotrexate, which interferes with folic acid metabolism, causing side effects such as hair loss and diarrhea. Folic acid deficiency may also result from heavy use of alcohol, which interferes with absorption of the vitamin. The oral administration of folic acid produces quick improvement in all symptoms. An adequate diet results in cure in cases due to simple malnutrition.

VITAMIN B12 DEFICIENCY

Deficiency of vitamin B12 (cobalamin), like folic acid, results in megaloblastic anemia, due to interference with normal DNA synthesis. Megaloblastic anemia is characterized by the production in the bone marrow of large, abnormal nucleated red cells known as megaloblasts. When vitamin B12 (or folic acid) deficiency occurs, bone marrow activity is seriously impaired. The marrow cells proliferate but do not mature properly, and erythropoiesis (the formation of new red blood cells) becomes largely ineffective. Anemia develops, the number of young red cells (reticulocytes) is reduced, and even the numbers of granulocytes (white cells that contain granules in the cellular substance outside the nucleus) and platelets are decreased. The mature red cells that are formed from megaloblasts are larger than normal, resulting in a macrocytic anemia. The impaired and ineffective erythropoiesis is associated with accelerated destruction of the red cells, thereby providing the features of a hemolytic anemia (caused by the destruction of red cells at a rate substantially greater than normal).

In pernicious anemia, the body's inability to absorb vitamin B12 is impaired, resulting in decreased production of red blood cells. Symptoms of pernicious anemia include weakness, waxy pallor, shortness of breath, rapid heartbeat, unsteady gait, smooth tongue, gastrointestinal disturbances, and neurological problems. Pernicious anemia is in most cases associated with an inflammation of the stomach called autoimmune gastritis. An absence of hydrochloric acid in gastric secretions (achlorhydria) is also characteristic of pernicious anemia. The anemia may become severe before the disorder is diagnosed because the vitamin deficiency develops very gradually.

In persons affected by pernicious anemia, vitamin B12 is unavailable due to a lack of intrinsic factor, a substance responsible for intestinal absorption of the vitamin. In a healthy person intrinsic factor is produced by the parietal cells of the stomach, the cells that also secrete hydrochloric acid. Intrinsic factor forms a complex with dietary vitamin B12 in the stomach. This complex remains intact, preventing degradation of the vitamin by intestinal juices, until it reaches the ileum of the small intestine, where the vitamin is released and absorbed into the body. When intrinsic factor is prevented from binding with vitamin B12 or when the parietal cells are unable to produce intrinsic factor, the vitamin is not absorbed and pernicious anemia results. This is believed to stem from an autoimmune reaction in which the malfunctioning immune system produces antibodies against intrinsic factor and against the parietal cells.

Pernicious anemia occurs most often in persons older than 30 years of age, although a juvenile form of the disease does occur, usually in children younger than 3 years of age. The disease shows a familial tendency and is more common in individuals of northern European descent.

Treatment involves a monthly intramuscular injection of vitamin B12 that must be continued for life. Injections or massive oral doses (1,000 µg) of vitamin may be needed. Most patients improve quickly, although neurological damage is seldom fully reversible and atrophy of the parietal cells and achlorhydria persist. Before the discovery of treatment in the 1920s, the modifier pernicious, although something of a misnomer today, was appropriate, since the disease was usually fatal.

Untreated vitamin B12 deficiency can result in nerve degeneration and eventually paralysis since the vitamin maintains the myelin sheath that protects nerve fibres. In some cases, large amounts of folic acid (over 1,000 μg per day) may conceal, and possibly even exacerbate, an underlying vitamin B12 deficiency.

Only animal foods are reliable sources of vitamin B12. Vegans, who eat no foods of animal origin, are at risk of vitamin B12 deficiency and must obtain the vitamin through fortified food or a supplement. For people who regularly eat animal products, deficiency of the vitamin is unlikely, unless there is a defect in absorption.

PANTOTHENIC ACID AND BIOTIN DEFICIENCIES

Pantothenic acid is so widespread in foods that deficiency is unlikely under normal circumstances. Deficiency has been seen only in individuals fed semisynthetic diets deficient in the vitamin or in subjects given a pantothenic acid antagonist. Symptoms of deficiency include fatigue, irritability, sleep disturbances, abdominal distress, and neurological symptoms such as tingling in the hands. Deficiency of the vitamin was suspected during World War II when prisoners of war in Asia who exhibited "burning feet" syndrome, characterized by numbness and tingling in the toes and other neurological symptoms, responded only to the administration of pantothenic acid.

Deficiency of biotin is rare, and this may be due in part to synthesis of the vitamin by bacteria in the colon, although the importance of this source is unclear. Biotin deficiency has been observed in people who regularly eat large quantities of raw egg white, which contains a glycoprotein (avidin) that binds biotin and prevents its absorption. A rare genetic defect that renders some infants unable to absorb a form of biotin in food can be treated with a supplement of the vitamin. Long-term use of certain anticonvulsant drugs may also impair biotin absorption. Symptoms of deficiency include skin rash, hair loss, and eventually neurological abnormalities.

VITAMIN C DEFICIENCY

Vitamin C deficiency is also known as scurvy, one of the oldest-known nutritional disorders of humankind. Vitamin C is important in the formation of collagen (an element of normal tissues), and any deficiency of the vitamin interferes with normal tissue synthesis, a problem that underlies the clinical manifestations of the disorder. Scurvy is characterized by swollen and bleeding gums with loosened teeth, soreness and stiffness of the joints and lower extremities, bleeding under the skin and in deep tissues, slow wound healing, and anemia.

Although accounts of what was probably scurvy are found in ancient writings, the first clear-cut descriptions appear in the records of the medieval Crusades. Later, toward the end of the 15th century, scurvy became the major cause of disability and mortality among sailors on long sea voyages. In 1753 Scottish naval surgeon James Lind showed that scurvy could be cured and prevented by ingestion of the juice of oranges and lemons. Soon citrus fruits became so common aboard ship that British sailors were referred to as "limeys."

In modern times, full-blown cases of vitamin C deficiency are relatively rare. They may still be seen in isolated elderly adults, in people following restrictive diets, and in infants fed reconstituted milk or milk substitutes without a vitamin C or orange juice supplement. Symptoms peculiar to

JAMES LIND

(b. 1716, Edinburgh, Scot.—d. July 13, 1794, Gosport, Hampshire, Eng.)

Scottish-born physician James Lind was known as the "founder of naval hygiene in England," a designation he earned through his recommendation that fresh citrus fruit and lemon juice be included in the diet of seamen. His recommendations eventually resulted in the eradication of scurvy from the British Navy.

A British naval surgeon (1739–48) and a physician at the Haslar Hospital for men of the Royal Navy, Gosport (1758–94), Lind observed thousands of cases of scurvy, typhus, and dysentery and the conditions on board ship that caused them. In 1754, when he published *A Treatise on Scurvy,* more British sailors were dying from scurvy during wartime than were killed in combat. In an early example of a clinical trial, Lind compared the effects of citrus fruits on patients with scurvy against five alternative remedies, showing that the fruit was noticeably better than vinegar, cider, seawater, and other remedies.

Nearly two centuries earlier the Dutch had discovered the benefits of citrus fruits and juices to sailors on long voyages. In his *Treatise* and in *On the Most Effectual Means of Preserving the Health of Seamen* (1757), Lind recommended this dietary practice. When it was finally adopted by the Royal Navy in 1795, scurvy disappeared from the ranks "as if by magic." Lind recommended shipboard delousing procedures, suggested the use of hospital ships for sick sailors in tropical ports, and arranged (1761) for the shipboard distillation of seawater for drinking. He also wrote *An Essay on Diseases Incidental to Europeans in Hot Climates* (1768).

infantile scurvy (Barlow's disease) include swelling and pain of the lower extremities and lesions of the growing bones.

Administration of vitamin C is the specific therapy for scurvy. Even in cases of severe deficiency, a daily dose of

100 mg for adults or 10 to 25 mg for infants and children, accompanied by a normal diet, commonly produces a cure within several days.

Disease states, environmental toxins, drugs, and other stresses can increase an individual's vitamin C needs. Smokers, for example, may require an additional 35 mg of the vitamin daily to maintain vitamin C levels comparable to nonsmokers.

VITAMIN TOXICITY

Because they can be stored in the liver and fatty tissue, fat-soluble vitamins, particularly vitamins A and D, have more potential for toxicity than do water-soluble vitamins, which, with the exception of vitamin B12, are readily excreted in the urine if taken in excess. Nonetheless, water-soluble vitamins can be toxic if taken as supplements or in fortified food.

Symptoms of acute vitamin A poisoning, which usually require a dose of at least 15,000 µg (50,000 IU) in adults, include abdominal pain, nausea, vomiting, headache, dizziness, blurred vision, and lack of muscular coordination. Chronic hypervitaminosis A, usually resulting from a sustained daily intake of 30,000 µg (100,000 IU) for months or years, may result in wide-ranging effects, including loss of bone density and liver damage. Vitamin A toxicity in young infants may be seen in a swelling of the fontanelles (soft spots) due to increased intracranial pressure. Large doses of vitamin A taken by a pregnant woman also can cause developmental abnormalities in a fetus, especially if taken during the first trimester; the precise threshold for causing birth defects is unknown, but less than 3,000 µg (10,000 IU) daily appears to be a safe intake. Although most vitamins occurring naturally in food do not cause adverse effects, toxic levels of vitamin A may be found in the liver of certain animals. For example, early Arctic explorers are reported to have been poisoned by eating polar bear liver. High beta-carotene intake, from supplements or from carrots or other foods that are high in beta-carotene, may after several weeks impart a yellowish cast to the skin but does not cause the same toxic effects as preformed vitamin A.

High intake of vitamin D can lead to a variety of debilitating effects, notably calcification of soft tissues and cardiovascular and renal damage. Although not a concern for most people, young children are especially vulnerable to vitamin D toxicity. Individuals with high intakes of fortified milk or fish or those who take many supplements may exceed the safe intake of 50 μg (2,000 IU) per day.

Because of its function as an antioxidant, supplementation with large doses (several hundred milligrams per day) of vitamin E in hopes of protecting against heart disease and other chronic diseases has become widespread. Such doses—many times the amount normally found in food—appear safe for most people, but their effectiveness in preventing disease or slowing the aging process has not been demonstrated. Daily intakes greater than 1,000 mg are not advised because they may interfere with blood clotting, causing hemorrhagic effects.

Large doses of niacin (nicotinic acid), given for its cholesterol-lowering effect, may produce a reddening of the skin, along with burning, tingling, and itching. Known as a "niacin flush," this is the first indicator of niacin excess, and this symptom is the basis for the safe daily intake of 35 mg. Liver toxicity and other adverse effects have also been reported with several grams of niacin a day.

Large doses of vitamin B6 have been taken in hopes of treating conditions such as carpal tunnel syndrome and premenstrual syndrome. The most critical adverse effect seen from such supplementation has been a severe sensory neuropathy of the extremities, including inability to walk. A daily intake of up to 100 mg is considered safe, although only 1 to 2 mg are required for good health.

Use of vitamin C supplements has been widespread since 1970, when chemist and Nobel laureate Linus Pauling suggested that the vitamin was protective against the common cold. Some studies have found a moderate benefit of vitamin C in reducing the duration and severity of common-cold episodes, but numerous studies have failed to find a significant effect on incidence. The most common side effect of high vitamin C intake is diarrhea and other gastrointestinal symptoms, likely due to the unabsorbed vitamin traversing the intestine. The safe intake of 2,000 mg a day is based on the avoidance of these gastrointestinal symptoms. Although other possible adverse effects of high vitamin C intake have been investigated, none has been demonstrated in healthy people.

CHAPTER 7

THE ROLE OF DIET IN CARDIOVASCULAR DISEASE AND CANCER

The relationship between diet and chronic disease (i.e., a disease that progresses over an extended period and does not resolve spontaneously) is complicated, not only because many diseases take years to develop but also because identifying a specific dietary cause is extremely difficult. Some prospective epidemiologic studies attempt to overcome this difficulty by following subjects for a number of years. Even then, the sheer complexity of the diet, as well as the multifactorial origins of chronic diseases, makes it difficult to prove causal links. Furthermore, many substances in food appear to act in a synergistic fashion—in the context of the whole diet rather than as individual agents—and single-agent studies may miss these interactive effects.

The concept of "risk factors" has been part of the public vocabulary for several decades, ever since the landmark Framingham Heart Study, begun in 1948, first reported in the early 1960s that cigarette smoking, elevated blood cholesterol, and high blood pressure were predictors of one's likelihood of dying from heart disease. Other studies confirmed and further elucidated these findings, and an extensive body of research has since shown that particular conditions or behaviours are strongly associated with specific diseases.

Not all individuals with a risk factor eventually develop a particular disease. However, the chance of developing the disease is greater when a known risk factor is present and increases further when several risk factors are present. Certain risk factors—such as diet, physical activity, and use of tobacco, alcohol, and other drugs—are modifiable, although it is often difficult to effect such change, even if one is facing possible disability or premature death. Others, including heredity, age, and sex, are not. Some risk factors are modifiable to varying degrees. These include exposure to sunlight and other forms of radiation, biological agents, and chemical agents (e.g., air and water pollution) that may play a role in causing genetic mutations that have been associated with increased risk of certain diseases, particularly cancer. Diet also has a fundamental impact on cardiovascular health, and many diseases of the cardiovascular system can be attributed to nutritional irregularities.

CARDIOVASCULAR DISEASE

Cardiovascular disease, a general term that encompasses diseases of the heart and blood vessels, is the leading cause of death in developed countries. Coronary heart disease (CHD), also known as coronary artery disease or ischemic heart disease, is the most common—and the most deadly—form of cardiovascular disease. CHD occurs when the arteries carrying blood to the heart, and thereby oxygen and nutrients, become narrow and obstructed. This narrowing is usually the result of atherosclerosis, a condition in which fibrous plaques (deposits of lipid and other material) build up on the inner walls of arteries, making them stiff and less responsive to changes in blood pressure. If blood flow is interrupted in the coronary arteries surrounding the heart, a myocardial infarction (heart attack) may occur. Restriction of blood flow to the brain due to a blood clot or hemorrhage may lead to a cerebrovascular accident, or stroke, and narrowing in the abdominal aorta, its major branches, or arteries of the legs may result in peripheral arterial disease. Most heart attacks and strokes are caused not by total blockage of the arteries by plaque but by blood clots that form more readily where small plaques are already partially blocking the arteries.

Although atherosclerosis typically takes decades to manifest in a heart attack or stroke, the disease may actually begin in childhood, with the appearance of fatty streaks, precursors to plaque. The deposition of plaque is, in essence, an inflammatory response directed at repairing injuries in the arterial wall. Smoking, hypertension, diabetes, and high blood levels of low-density lipoprotein (LDL) cholesterol are among the many factors associated with vessel injury. Infection by certain bacteria or viruses may also contribute to inflammation and vessel damage. Particularly vulnerable to premature CHD are middle-aged men, especially those with a family history of the disease, and individuals with hereditary conditions such as familial hypercholesterolemias.

Diet and weight loss are influential in modifying four major risk factors for CHD: high levels of LDL cholesterol, low levels of high-density lipoprotein (HDL) cholesterol, hypertension, and diabetes. However, the role of diet in influencing the established risk factors is not as clear as the role of the risk factors themselves in CHD. Furthermore, dietary strategies are most useful when combined with other approaches, such as smoking cessation and regular exercise. Drug therapy may include cholesterol-lowering drugs such as statins, bile acid sequestrants, and niacin, as well as aspirin or anticoagulants to prevent formation of blood clots and antihypertensive medication to lower blood pressure. Although endogenous estrogen (that produced by the body) is thought to confer protection against

CHD in premenopausal women, recent studies call into question the value of hormone therapy in reducing CHD risk in women who have gone through menopause.

HYPERTENSION

Hypertension, or high blood pressure, is one of the most common health problems in developed countries. It is an important risk factor for other diseases, such as CHD, congestive heart failure, stroke, aneurysm, and kidney disease. Most people with high blood pressure have essential, or primary, hypertension, for which no specific cause can be determined. Heredity plays a role in the development of the disease, but so do modifiable factors such as excess weight, physical inactivity, high alcohol intake, and diets high in salt. For reasons that are not entirely clear, African Americans have among the highest rates of hypertension in the world.

Hypertension is usually defined as a blood pressure equal to or greater than 140/90 mm Hg—equivalent to the pressure exerted by a column of mercury 140 mm high during contraction of the heart (systole) and 90 mm high during relaxation (diastole). Either systolic or diastolic blood pressure, or both, may be elevated in hypertension. Individuals with hypertension can be asymptomatic for years and then suddenly experience a fatal stroke or heart attack. Prevention and management of hypertension can significantly decrease the chance of complications. Early identification of hypertension is important so that lifestyle modification can begin as early as possible.

Overweight people, especially those with excess abdominal fat, have a much greater risk of developing hypertension than do lean people. Weight loss alone, sometimes as little as 10 pounds (4.5 kg), can be extremely effective in reducing high blood pressure.

Increasing physical activity can, of course, help with weight control, but it also appears to lower blood pressure independently.

Large studies examining salt intake and blood pressure in communities around the world have clearly established that blood pressure is positively related to dietary intake of sodium (salt). Primitive societies in which sodium intake is low have very little hypertension, and the increase in blood pressure that typically occurs with age in industrialized societies fails to occur. On the other hand, in countries with extremely high salt consumption, hypertension is common and stroke is a leading cause of death. Furthermore, experimental studies indicate that decreasing sodium intake can reduce blood pressure.

Some people appear to be genetically sensitive to salt. Although salt restriction may only help lower blood pressure in those who are salt sensitive, many individuals consume more salt than is needed. Dietary recommendations typically encourage the general population to limit sodium intake to no more than 2,400 mg daily, which amounts to a little more than a teaspoon of salt. This level can be achieved by restricting salt used in cooking, not adding salt at the table, and limiting highly salted foods, processed foods (many of which have hidden sodium), and so-called fast foods. Canned vegetables, breakfast cereals, and luncheon meats are particularly high in sodium.

Heavy alcohol consumption (more than two drinks a day) is associated with hypertension. Vegetarians, and particularly vegans (who consume no foods of animal origin, including milk and eggs), tend to have lower blood pressure than do meat eaters. The diet recommended for reducing blood pressure, which will also benefit cardiovascular health, emphasizes fruits, vegetables, and low-fat dairy products; includes whole grains, poultry, fish, and nuts; and contains only small amounts of red meat and sugary foods and beverages. Reducing salt intake should further increase the effectiveness of the diet.

A variety of drugs is used to treat hypertension, some of which have nutritional repercussions. Thiazide diuretics, for example, increase potassium loss from the body, usually necessitating the intake of additional potassium, which is particularly plentiful in foods such as bananas, citrus fruits, vegetables, and potatoes. Use of potassium-based salt substitutes is not advised without medical supervision.

METABOLIC SYNDROME

Metabolic syndrome, also called Syndrome X, is characterized by a cluster of metabolic abnormalities associated with an increased risk for CHD, diabetes, stroke, and certain types of cancer. The condition was first named Syndrome X in 1988 by American endocrinologist Gerald Reaven, who identified insulin resistance and a subset of secondary conditions as major risk factors for CHD. The diagnosis of metabolic syndrome requires the presence of multiple—typically at least three—CHD risk factors, which include abdominal obesity, decreased levels of HDL cholesterol, elevated blood triglycerides, high blood pressure, and insulin resistance. Other indications associated with the syndrome include elevated levels of C-reactive protein, a substance involved in mediating systemic inflammatory responses, and elevated levels of fibrinogen, a protein essential for the formation of blood clots.

Metabolic syndrome is common, affecting nearly 25 percent of adults in the United States and the United Kingdom, with the prevalence of the condition being especially high in adults over age 60 and in individuals who are overweight or obese. Insulin resistance, which is believed to play a central role in metabolic syndrome, renders

DEAN ORNISH

(b. July 16, 1953, Dallas, Texas, U.S.)

American physician Dean Ornish became best known for his approach to treating heart disease through radical diet modification and exercise, which generated significant debate in the medical community and attracted a popular following.

Ornish was raised in Dallas by his father, a dentist, and his mother, a children's book author and film-maker. He attended Rice University in Houston but dropped out after experiencing severe depression and mononucleosis. Ornish eventually received a bachelor's degree in humanities (1975) from the University of Texas at Austin,

Dr. Dean Ornish. Michael Tullberg/Getty Images

graduating first in his class. He received an M.D. (1980) in internal medicine from Baylor College of Medicine in Houston. Ornish then moved to the Boston area for a clinical fellowship at Harvard Medical School and an internship and residency in internal medicine at Massachusetts General Hospital, which he completed in 1984.

Ornish moved to San Francisco in July 1984 after accepting a teaching position at the University of California School of Medicine. That year Ornish also founded the nonprofit Preventive Medicine Research Institute (PMRI) in nearby Sausalito. He began the Lifestyle Heart Trial, a controlled study of the effects of a low-fat diet and stress-management regime on a small group of heart-disease patients, implementing a unique approach to treating heart disease that he developed in the late 1970s while he was still a student. The diet limited fats to 10 percent of total caloric intake and cholesterol to only 5 mg a day, mainly through eliminating animal products and processed foods. (In contrast, the recommendations of the American Heart Association allow up to 30 percent of total calories from fat and 300 mg of cholesterol daily.) In addition to giving up smoking and fatty foods, the test subjects did yoga, meditated, and participated in a support group. Ornish believed that the stress-management aspect of his program, designed to combat social isolation as well as daily pressures, was as essential to his patients' recovery as diet and physical activity.

The results of the trial, published in 1990, revealed that at least some effects of coronary atherosclerosis had been reversed in many patients. Major insurers and Medicare subsequently agreed to cover the cost of participation in Ornish's program, which did not use the medications and surgical procedures typical of standard treatment. But some medical experts expressed skepticism about the likelihood that patients in this program, and a later one Ornish developed for prostate cancer, would remain healthy once free of his supervision. They likewise questioned the validity of his studies.

Ornish was a physician consultant to Pres. Bill Clinton from 1993 to 2000 and was appointed to the White House Commission on Complementary and Alternative Medicine Policy in 2001. He wrote several popular books during his career, including *Stress, Diet, and Your Heart* (1982) and *The Spectrum: A Scientifically Proven Program to Feel Better, Live Longer, Lose Weight, and Gain Health* (2007).

tissues insensitive to insulin and therefore unable to store glucose. Insulin resistance can be caused by obesity, lipodystrophy (atrophy of adipose tissue resulting in fat deposition in nonadipose tissues), physical inactivity, and genetic factors. Furthermore, metabolic syndrome can be exacerbated by poor diet (e.g., excessive carbohydrate or fat consumption) in susceptible people and has been associated with Stein-Leventhal syndrome (also called polycystic ovary syndrome), sleep apnea, and fatty liver.

Individuals with metabolic syndrome benefit from regular physical activity and weight reduction, along with a diet low in carbohydrates and saturated fat and enriched with unsaturated fat. Patients with moderate to severe symptoms may require treatment with drugs. For example, high blood pressure may be treated with antihypertensive drugs, such as angiotensin-converting enzyme inhibitors (e.g., lisinopril) or diuretics (e.g., chlorthalidone), and patients with high cholesterol levels may be treated with statins or nicotinic acid. In addition, patients at high risk of heart disease may benefit from low-dose aspirin to prevent blood clots, whereas those at high risk of diabetes may require injections of insulin or administration of metformin to lower blood glucose levels.

BLOOD LIPOPROTEINS

Because lipids such as cholesterol, triglycerides, and phospholipids are nonpolar and insoluble in water, they must be bound to proteins, forming complex particles called lipoproteins, to be transported in the watery medium of blood. LDLs, which are the main transporters of cholesterol in the blood, carry cholesterol from the liver to body cells, including those in the arteries, where it can contribute to plaque. Multiple lines of evidence point to high levels of LDL cholesterol as causal in the development of CHD, and LDL is the main blood lipoprotein targeted by intervention efforts. Furthermore, clinical trials have demonstrated that LDL-lowering therapy reduces heart attacks and strokes in people who already have CHD.

HDLs, on the other hand, are thought to transport excess cholesterol to the liver for removal, thereby helping to prevent plaque formation. HDL cholesterol is inversely correlated with CHD risk, and therefore intervention efforts aim to increase HDL cholesterol levels. Another blood lipoprotein form, the very-low-density lipoprotein (VLDL), is also an independent CHD risk factor, but to a lesser extent than LDL and HDL. As the major carrier of triglyceride (fat) in the blood, VLDL is particularly elevated in people who are overweight and in those with diabetes and metabolic syndrome.

Although LDL cholesterol is popularly referred to as "bad" cholesterol and HDL cholesterol is often called "good" cholesterol, it is actually the lipoprotein form—not the cholesterol being carried in the lipoprotein—that is related to CHD risk. Total cholesterol levels, which are highly correlated with LDL cholesterol levels, are typically used for initial screening purposes, although a complete lipoprotein evaluation is more revealing. A desirable blood lipid profile is a total cholesterol level below 200 mg per decilitre (mg/dl), an HDL cholesterol level of at least 40 mg/dl, a fasting triglyceride level of less than 150 mg/dl, and an LDL cholesterol level below 100, 130, or 160 mg/dl, depending on degree of heart attack risk.

DIETARY FAT

It is widely accepted that a low-fat diet lowers blood cholesterol and is protective against heart disease. Also, a high-fat intake is often, although not always, linked to obesity, which in turn can increase heart disease risk. Yet, the situation is complicated by the fact that different fatty acids have differing effects on the various lipoproteins that carry cholesterol. Furthermore, when certain fats are lowered in the diet, they may be replaced by other components that carry risk. High-carbohydrate diets, for example, may actually increase cardiovascular risk for some individuals, such as those prone to metabolic syndrome or type 2 diabetes. Heredity also plays a role in an individual's response to particular dietary manipulations.

In general, saturated fatty acids, which are found primarily in animal foods, tend to elevate LDL and total blood cholesterol. However, the most cholesterol-raising saturated fatty acids (lauric, myristic, and palmitic acids) can come from both plant and animal sources, while stearic acid, derived from animal fat as well as from cocoa butter, is considered neutral, neither raising nor lowering blood cholesterol levels.

When saturated fatty acids are replaced by unsaturated fatty acids—either monounsaturated or poly-unsaturated—LDL and total blood cholesterol are usually lowered, an effect largely attributed to the reduction in saturated fat. However, polyunsaturated fatty acids tend to lower HDL cholesterol levels, while monounsaturated fatty acids tend to maintain them. The major monounsaturated fatty acid in animals and plants is oleic acid, good dietary sources of which are olive, canola, and high-oleic safflower oils, as well as avocados, nuts, and seeds. Historically, the low mortality from CHD in populations eating a traditional Mediterranean diet has been linked to the high consumption of olive oil in the region, although the plentiful supply of fruits and vegetables could also be a factor.

The two types of polyunsaturated fatty acids found in foods are omega-3 fatty acids and omega-6 fatty acids. Linoleic acid, the primary omega-6 fatty acid in most diets, is widespread in foods. Its major source is vegetable oils such as sunflower, safflower, and corn oils. Low cardiovascular disease rates in Eskimo populations eating traditional diets high in omega-3 fatty acids initially provoked the speculation that these fatty acids may be protective against CHD. The primary lipid-altering effect of omega-3 fatty acids is the reduction of blood triglycerides. Omega-3 fatty acids may also protect the heart and blood vessels by lowering blood pressure, reducing blood clotting, preventing irregular heart rhythms, and acting as anti-inflammatory agents. The long-chain omega-3 fatty acids eicosapentaenoic acid (EPA) and docosahexaenoic acid (DHA) are derived from alpha-linolenic acid, a shorter-chain member of the same family. Fatty fish such as salmon, herring, sardines, mackerel, and tuna are high in both EPA and DHA. Flaxseed is an excellent source of alpha-linolenic acid, which the body can convert to the long-chain omega-3 fatty acids. Other sources of omega-3 fatty acids include walnuts, hazelnuts, almonds, canola oil, soybean oil, dark green leafy vegetables such as spinach, and egg yolk. A diet high in polyunsaturated fatty acids may increase LDL lipid oxidation and thereby accelerate atherosclerosis. Therefore, such a diet should be accompanied by increased intakes of vitamin E, an antioxidant. Fish oil supplements are not advised without medical supervision because of possible adverse effects, such as bleeding.

The safety of *trans* (as opposed to naturally occurring *cis*) unsaturated fatty acids has been called into question because *trans*-fatty acids in the diet raise LDL cholesterol to about the same extent as do saturated fatty acids, and they can also lower HDL cholesterol. Trans-fatty acids are found naturally in some animal fats, such as beef, butter, and milk, but they are also produced during the hydrogenation process, in which unsaturated oils are made harder and more stable. Certain margarines, snack foods, baked goods, and deep-fried products are major food sources of *trans*-fatty acids.

DIETARY CHOLESTEROL

Cholesterol in food and cholesterol in the blood are distinct entities, and they are often confused. Dietary cholesterol is found only in foods of animal origin, and it is particularly high in egg yolk and organ meats. Cholesterol in the diet raises LDL cholesterol but not as much as saturated fatty acids do. If dietary cholesterol is already high, consuming even more cholesterol may not increase blood cholesterol levels further because of feedback control mechanisms. Also, there is great individual variation in response to dietary cholesterol. For healthy people, a cholesterol intake averaging less than 300 mg daily is recommended. However, because cholesterol is synthesized by the body, none is required in the diet.

OTHER DIETARY FACTORS

Ingestion of soluble fibre, a component of dietary fibre (indigestible plant material), lowers LDL and total blood cholesterol levels and has been linked to decreased mortality from cardiovascular disease. Sources of soluble fibre include whole oats, barley, legumes, some vegetables, and fruits, particularly apples, plums, apricots, blueberries, strawberries, and citrus fruits. Psyllium and other fibre supplements may also be recommended. The mechanism whereby soluble fibre lowers cholesterol levels is unclear, although it is probably related to its ability to bind with cholesterol and bile acids in the gut, thereby removing them from circulation. Other factors may contribute as well, such as fermentation of fibre by bacteria in the colon, resulting in compounds that inhibit cholesterol synthesis.

Light to moderate alcohol intake (up to two drinks per day for men and one drink per day for women) is associated with reduced CHD risk, primarily because of its ability to raise HDL cholesterol levels and possibly because it helps prevent blood clot formation. Alcohol intake may help explain the so-called French paradox: heart disease rates in France are low despite a CHD risk profile comparable to that in the United States, where rates are relatively high. Wine also contains antioxidant compounds, such as resveratrol from grape skins, that may inhibit LDL oxidation, but the beneficial effect of these substances is likely far less than that of alcohol itself.

Mortality from stroke and heart disease is significantly associated with dietary sodium (salt) intake, but only in overweight individuals, who may have an increased sensitivity to dietary sodium. Sodium intake also appears to have a direct effect on risk of stroke beyond its effect on blood pressure, which itself influences stroke risk. On the other hand, diets rich in potassium are linked to reduced risk of stroke.

Soy foods are associated with decreased LDL and total blood cholesterol levels, as well as other vascular effects associated with reduced CHD risk. Tofu, tempeh, miso, soy flour, soy milk, and soy nuts are among the soy foods that contain isoflavones, estrogen-like compounds that are thought to be responsible for these beneficial cardio-vascular effects.

Antioxidant substances found in food and taken as dietary supplements include vitamin C, vitamin E, and beta-carotene (a plant precursor to vitamin A). Dietary antioxidants may lower CHD risk, although clinical trials have not yet supported this notion.

OTHER FACTORS

For blood pressure that is equal to or greater than the "pre-hypertension" level of 120/80 millimetres of mercury (mm Hg), the more elevated the blood pressure, the greater the risk of heart disease. Hypertension (140/90 mm Hg and above) and atherosclerosis are mutually reinforcing: hypertension injures artery walls, thereby encouraging plaque formation; and once plaque has formed and arteries are less elastic, hypertension is aggravated. If hypertension is treated, the incidence of CHD, stroke, and congestive heart failure decreases.

Diabetes—often accompanied by hypertension, high blood triglyceride levels, and obesity—is an important risk factor for heart disease and also warrants aggressive intervention. Furthermore, for people with diabetes who have a heart attack, there is an unusually high death rate, immediately or in the ensuing years. If blood glucose levels are strictly controlled, vascular complications will be decreased.

Obesity is also an important factor in cardiovascular disease, primarily through its influence on other simultaneously present risk factors. Obese individuals often have an abnormal glucose tolerance and diabetes, hypertension, and blood lipoprotein abnormalities, including higher triglyceride levels and lower HDL cholesterol levels. Fat accumulation around the waist (the so-called apple shape) puts one at greater risk for premature heart disease than does fat accumulation around the hips (pear shape). A waist circumference greater than 40 inches (102 cm) for men or 35 inches (88 cm) for women is considered a high risk. Besides helping to control weight, regular exercise is thought to decrease CHD risk in several ways: slowing the progression of atherosclerosis, increasing the blood supply to the heart muscle, increasing HDL cholesterol, reducing VLDL levels, improving glucose tolerance, and reducing blood pressure. At a minimum, 30 minutes of moderate aerobic activity, such as brisk walking, on most days is recommended.

Individuals with the genetic disease hereditary hemochromatosis excessively absorb iron, which can build up to dangerously high levels and damage the heart, liver, and other organs. Approximately 1 in 9 people of European descent are carriers (i.e., have one of two possible genes) for the disease and have an increased risk of heart disease. However, studies examining the possible role of dietary iron in heart disease risk for those who lack the gene for hemochromatosis have been inconclusive.

The amino acid homocysteine, when present in elevated amounts in blood, may damage arteries and promote atherosclerosis. Inadequate intake of vitamin B6, vitamin B12, or folic acid can increase blood homocysteine levels, although folic acid deficiency is the most common cause. While elevated homocysteine is not yet an established risk factor for CHD, it is prudent to ensure adequate intake of folic acid.

CANCER

Second only to cardiovascular disease as a cause of death in much of the world, cancer is the major killer of adults ages 45 and older. The various types of cancer differ not only in location in the body and affected cell type but also in the course of the disease, treatments, and suspected causal or contributory factors.

Studies of identical twins reveal that, even for those with an identical genetic makeup, the risk for most cancers is still largely related to environmental factors. Another line of evidence supporting the limited role of heredity in most cancers is studies of migrant populations, in which cancer rates tend to grow more like a group's adopted country with each passing generation. For example, rates of breast and colorectal cancers in individuals who migrate from rural Asia to the United States gradually increase to match the higher cancer rates of the United States. On the other hand, risk of stomach cancer gradually decreases after Japanese migrants move to the United States. Nutrition is among the critical environmental and lifestyle factors investigated in migration studies, although identifying specific dietary components that affect the changing disease rates has been more elusive. A number of cancer organizations around the world have estimated that 30 to 40 percent of all cases of cancer could be prevented by appropriate dietary means.

Most cancer-causing substances (carcinogens) probably enter the body through the alimentary canal in food and beverages. Although some foodborne toxins, pesticides, and food additives may be carcinogenic if taken in sufficient quantity, it is primarily the foodstuffs themselves that are associated with cancer. Some dietary patterns or components may promote cancer, while others may inhibit it. Substances in the diet, or other environmental factors, can act anywhere along the multistage process of cancer development (carcinogenesis): initiation, in which DNA, the genetic material in a cell, is altered; promotion, in which cells with altered DNA multiply; and progression, in which cancer cells spread to surrounding tissue and distant sites (metastasis).

Studies attempting to relate total fat or specific types of fat to various cancers have been inconsistent. High intake of dietary fat may promote cancer, but this could be due at least in part to the extra energy (calories) that fat provides. Obesity is associated with several types of cancer, including colorectal, prostate, uterine, pancreatic, and breast cancers. A possible mechanism for this effect is the higher circulating levels of estrogen, insulin, and other hormones that accompany increased body fat. Furthermore, regular exercise has been shown in a number of studies to reduce the risk of breast and colon cancers. In laboratory animals, restricting energy intake is the most effective method for reducing cancer risk. Chronic underfeeding inhibits the growth of many spontaneous tumours and most experimentally induced tumours.

High alcohol consumption is another factor that has been implicated in the development of various cancers, especially of the mouth, throat, liver, and esophagus (where it acts synergistically with tobacco) and probably of the breast, colon, and rectum. The fact that moderate use of alcohol has a beneficial effect on cardiovascular disease underscores how complex and potentially confusing is the connection between food and health.

Foods also contain substances that offer some protection against cancer. For example, fresh fruits and vegetables, and specifically vitamins C and E, eaten at the same time as nitrate-containing foods (such as ham, bacon, sausages, frankfurters, and luncheon meats), inhibit nitrosamine production and thus help protect against stomach cancer. Several hundred studies have found a strong association between diets high in vegetables and fruits and lower risk for various cancers, although identifying specific protective factors in such diets has been more difficult. Vitamin C, vitamin E, carotenoids such as beta-carotene (a plant precursor of vitamin A), and the trace mineral selenium act in the body's antioxidant systems to help prevent DNA damage by reactive molecules known as free radicals. Specific vegetables, notably the cruciferous vegetables (broccoli, cauliflower, Brussels sprouts, kale, and other members of the cabbage family), contain sulforaphane and other compounds known as isothiocyanates, which induce enzymes that detoxify carcinogens and have been demonstrated to protect against cancer in animal studies. Dietary fibre in plant foods may also be protective: it dilutes potential carcinogens, binds to them, and speeds up transit time through the gut, thereby limiting exposure. Fruits and vegetables are rich in phytochemicals (biologically active plant substances), which

A woman drinking green tea during a tea ceremony in Kobe, Japan. Tea contains antioxidants called polyphenols, which may curb the growth of certain types of cancers. Buddhika Weerasinghe/Getty Images

are currently being investigated for potential anticarcinogenic activity. Animal studies suggest that antioxidant compounds known as polyphenols, which are found in both black and green tea, may be protective against the growth of cancer. Regular consumption of tea, especially in Japan and China, where green tea is the preferred type, has been associated with a decreased risk of various cancers, especially stomach cancer, but the evidence has been conflicting.

The dietary approach most likely to reduce cancer risk is one that is rich in foods from plant sources, such as fruits, vegetables (especially cruciferous ones), whole grains, beans, and nuts; has a limited intake of fat, especially animal fat; includes a balance of energy intake and physical activity to maintain a healthy body weight; and includes alcohol in moderation, if at all. Intake of carcinogenic compounds can also be reduced by trimming fat and removing burned portions from meat before eating.

COLORECTAL CANCER

Consumption of meat, particularly red meat and processed meat, is associated with a modest increase in risk of colorectal cancer. However, it is unclear whether this effect is related to a specific component of meat; to the fact that other nutrients, such as fibre, may be in short supply in a high-meat diet; or to carcinogenic substances, such as heterocyclic amines and polycyclic aromatic hydrocarbons, which are produced during high-temperature grilling and broiling, particularly of fatty muscle meats. High alcohol consumption and low intakes of calcium and folic acid have also been linked to an increased rate of colorectal cancer.

Although fibre-rich foods also appear to be protective against colorectal cancer in many studies, attempts to demonstrate a specific protective effect of dietary fibre, distinct from the nonfibre constituents of vegetables and fruits, have been inconclusive. Obesity is an important risk factor for colorectal cancer in men and premenopausal women, and mild or moderate physical activity is strongly associated with a decreased risk of colon cancer.

PROSTATE CANCER

There is a growing body of evidence that a diet low in fat and animal products and rich in fruits and vegetables, including the cruciferous type, is protective against prostate cancer. This protection may be partially explained by a fibre found in fruits and vegetables called pectin, which has been shown to possess anticancer properties. Lower prostate cancer risk has been associated with the consumption of tomatoes and tomato products, which are rich sources of the carotenoid antioxidant lycopene. Prostate cancer rates are low in countries such as Japan where soy foods are consumed regularly, but there is no direct evidence that soy protects against the disease. The possible protective effect against prostate cancer of vitamin E and the mineral selenium is under investigation.

BREAST CANCER

The relationship between diet and breast cancer is unclear. High-fat diets have been suspected of contributing to breast cancer, based on international correlations between fat intake and breast cancer rates, as well as animal studies. However, large prospective studies have not confirmed this connection, even though a diet high in fat may be inadvisable for other reasons. Similarly, a diet high in fruits and vegetables is certainly healthful but provides no known protection against breast cancer. Alcohol intake is associated with breast cancer, but the increased risk appears related only to heavy drinking. Lifelong regular exercise may be protective against breast cancer, possibly because it helps to control weight, and obesity is associated with increased risk of postmenopausal breast cancer. Heredity and levels of estrogen over the course of a lifetime are the primary established influences on breast cancer risk.

Enthusiasm for soy foods and soy products as protection against breast cancer has been growing in recent years in the industrialized world. Although Japanese women, who have low breast cancer rates, have a lifelong exposure to high dietary soy, their situation is not necessarily comparable to midlife supplementation with soy isoflavones (estrogen-like compounds) in Western women. Isoflavones appear to compete with estrogen (e.g., in premenopausal women), and thereby blunt its effect. When in a low-estrogen environment (e.g., in postmenopausal women) they exert weak estrogenic effects. There is as yet no consistent evidence that soy in the diet offers protection against breast cancer or any other cancer, and the effects of dietary soy once cancer has been initiated are unknown (estrogen itself is a cancer promoter). Ongoing research on the benefits of soy is promising, and consumption of soy foods such as tofu is encouraged, but consumption of isolated soy constituents such as isoflavones, which have unknown risks, is not warranted.

CHAPTER 8

THE ROLE OF DIET IN DIABETES AND GASTROINTESTINAL HEALTH

Obesity and diabetes are major health threats in countries worldwide, and both have direct associations with diet, namely the overconsumption of food. The prevalence of other eating disorders, including anorexia nervosa and bulimia nervosa, suggests that many people struggle with regulating their food intake and maintaining a healthy diet. But while diet plays a major role in the onset of these disorders, it also serves a central role in their treatment. Likewise, diet is closely associated with gastrointestinal health, influencing the onset and intensity of conditions such as heartburn, peptic ulcers, and inflammatory bowel disease, as well as facilitating their treatment.

DIABETES MELLITUS AND METABOLIC DISORDERS

Diabetes mellitus is a group of metabolic disorders of carbohydrate metabolism characterized by high blood glucose levels (hyperglycemia) and usually resulting from insufficient production of the hormone insulin (type 1 diabetes) or an ineffective response of cells to insulin (type 2 diabetes). Secreted by the pancreas, insulin is required to transport blood glucose (sugar) into cells. Diabetes is an important risk factor for cardiovascular disease, as well as

A young boy with diabetes injecting himself with insulin. The hormone insulin is vital to balancing a person's blood glucose levels. Science Photo Library/Getty Images

a leading cause of adult blindness. Other long-term complications include kidney failure, nerve damage, and lower limb amputation due to impaired circulation.

Type 1 diabetes (formerly known as juvenile-onset or insulin-dependent diabetes) can occur at any age but often begins in late childhood with the pancreas failing to secrete adequate amounts of insulin. Type 1 diabetes has a strong genetic link, but most cases are the result of an autoimmune disorder, possibly set off by a viral infection, foreign protein, or environmental toxin. Although elevated blood sugar is an important feature of diabetes, sugar or carbohydrate in the diet is not the cause of the disease. Type 1 diabetes is managed by injections of insulin, along with small, regularly spaced meals and snacks that spread glucose intake throughout the day and minimize fluctuations in blood glucose.

Type 2 diabetes (formerly known as adult-onset or non-insulin-dependent diabetes) is the more common type of diabetes, constituting 90 to 95 percent of cases. With this condition, insulin resistance renders cells unable to admit glucose, which then accumulates in the blood. Although type 2 diabetes generally starts in middle age, it is increasingly reported in childhood, especially in obese children. Genetic susceptibility to this form of diabetes may not be expressed unless a person has excess body fat, especially abdominal obesity. Weight loss often helps to normalize blood glucose regulation, and oral antidiabetic agents may also be used. Lifestyle intervention (e.g., diet and exercise) is highly effective in delaying or preventing type 2 diabetes in high-risk individuals.

Migration studies have shown that urbanization and adoption of a Western diet and habits can dramatically increase the rate of type 2 diabetes. For example, a high prevalence of the disorder is seen in the Pima Indians of Arizona, who are sedentary and eat a high-fat diet, whereas prevalence is low in a closely related group of Pimas living a traditional lifestyle—physically active, with lower body weight and a diet that is lower in fat—in a remote, mountainous region of Mexico. Type 2 diabetes is a serious health problem among Native Americans and other ethnic minorities in the United States. Worldwide, the prevalence of type 2 diabetes has increased sharply, along with the rise in obesity.

Specific treatment plans for diabetics are designed after individual medical assessment and consultation with a registered dietitian or qualified nutrition professional. The therapeutic diet, which has changed considerably over the years, focuses on complex carbohydrates, dietary fibre (particularly the soluble type), and regulated proportions of carbohydrate, protein, and fat. Because heart disease is the leading cause of death among diabetics, saturated fatty acids and *trans*-fatty acids are also restricted, and physical activity and weight control are strongly encouraged. Older dietary recommendations restricted sugar in the diabetic diet, but recent guidelines allow a moderate intake of sugars, so long as other carbohydrates are reduced in the same meal. Diet and exercise are also used to manage a condition known as gestational diabetes, which develops in a small percentage of pregnant women and usually resolves itself after delivery, though such women are subsequently at increased risk of developing type 2 diabetes.

Research in the 1990s led to the development of a new tool, the glycemic index, which reflects the finding that different carbohydrate foods have effects on blood glucose levels that cannot be predicted on the basis of their chemical structure. For example, the simple sugars formed from digestion of some starchy foods, such as bread or potatoes, are absorbed more quickly and cause a faster rise in blood glucose than does table sugar (sucrose), fruit, or milk. In practical terms, however, if a carbohydrate food is eaten as part of a mixed meal, its so-called glycemic effect is less consequential. The glycemic index may prove to be a useful option for planning diabetic diets, but it in no way obviates the need for other established therapeutic practices, such as limiting total carbohydrate intake and managing body weight.

The trace element chromium is a cofactor for insulin and is important for glucose tolerance. Malnourished infants with impaired glucose tolerance have been shown to benefit from additional chromium, but there is no evidence that most people with diabetes are deficient in chromium or in need of chromium supplementation.

If a diabetic injects too much insulin, blood glucose may drop to dangerously low levels. The irritability, shakiness, sweating, headache, and confusion that ensue are indicative of low blood sugar, known as hypoglycemia. Severe hypoglycemia, if untreated, can lead to seizures, coma, and even death. Reactive hypoglycemia of nondiabetic origin is a distinct disorder of carbohydrate metabolism in which blood glucose falls unduly (below 50 mg/dl) after an overproduction of the body's own insulin in response to a meal high in simple sugars. Symptoms of hypoglycemia occur simultaneously. However, this condition is uncommon.

Numerous inherited metabolic disorders, also known as inborn errors of metabolism, respond to dietary treatment. Most of these relatively rare disorders are inherited as autosomal recessive traits (i.e., both parents must be carriers) and result in a specific enzyme or cofactor that has reduced activity or is absent altogether. Biochemical pathways of amino acid, carbohydrate, or fatty acid metabolism may be affected, each having a number of possible enzyme defects. In some cases, newborn screening programs, and even prenatal diagnosis, allow for early identification and successful intervention. Without prompt and aggressive

HYPOGLYCEMIA

Hypoglycemia is a reduction of the concentration of glucose in the blood below normal levels, commonly occurring as a complication of treatment for diabetes mellitus. In healthy individuals an intricate glucoregulatory system acts rapidly to counter hypoglycemia by reducing insulin production (insulin is important in the mechanism that removes glucose from the bloodstream) and mobilizing energy reserves from the fat and liver. When this regulatory system does not operate, disproportionately large amounts of insulin in the blood result in sudden drastic falls in circulating glucose.

The manifestations of hypoglycemia evolve in a characteristic pattern. Mild hypoglycemia—for example, blood glucose concentrations less than 55 mg per 100 ml (3 mmol/l)—causes hunger, fatigue, tremour, rapid pulse, and anxiety. These symptoms are known as sympathoadrenal symptoms because they are caused by activation of the sympathetic nervous system, including the adrenal medulla. Activation of the sympathetic nervous system increases blood glucose concentrations by mobilizing liver glycogen, which is the principal storage form of carbohydrate in liver and muscle. More severe hypoglycemia—for example, blood glucose concentrations less than 45 mg per 100 ml (2.5 mmol/l)—causes blurred vision, impaired thinking and consciousness, confusion, seizures, and coma. These symptoms are known as neuroglycopenic symptoms because they are indicative of glucose deprivation in the brain. Sympathoadrenal symptoms and neuroglycopenic symptoms are nonspecific and should be attributed to hypoglycemia only when relieved by either oral or intravenous administration of glucose.

The principal causes of hypoglycemia can be grouped into two categories: insulin-dependent and insulin-independent. Insulin-dependent hypoglycemia is caused by too much insulin (hyperinsulinemia), usually attributed to the intake of a sulfonylurea drug or to the presence of excess insulin in a patient with diabetes. Other, much less common causes of insulin-dependent hypoglycemia may include an insulin-secreting tumour of the islets of Langerhans (in the pancreas) or a tumour, usually of fibrous tissue, that secretes insulin-like growth factor 2 (IGF-2), which activates insulin receptors. Insulin-independent hypoglycemia is caused by disorders that result in impaired glucose mobilization during fasting (defects in gluconeogenesis or glycogenolysis). Impaired glucose mobilization may be caused by adrenal insufficiency, severe liver disease, glycogen storage disease, severe infections, and starvation. Insulin-dependent hypoglycemia is diagnosed by an inappropriately high serum insulin concentration when symptoms of hypoglycemia are present. Conversely, insulin-independent hypoglycemia is diagnosed by an inappropriately low serum insulin concentration when symptoms of hypoglycemia are present.

Many people have hypoglycemia-like symptoms three to five hours after a meal. However, few of these people have hypoglycemia when symptomatic, and their symptoms may not improve with the administration of glucose. Symptoms can often be controlled by eating small snacks every few hours, exercising regularly, and managing weight. A known cause of post-meal hypoglycemia is gastrectomy (removal of the stomach) or gastric bypass surgery for obesity, which results in rapid absorption of glucose into the blood, thereby triggering excessive insulin secretion and hypoglycemia.

treatment, most of these disorders have a poor prognosis, resulting in severe intellectual disorders and other forms of illness. Phenylketonuria (PKU), a condition in which the amino acid phenylalanine is not properly metabolized to the amino acid tyrosine, is the most recognized of these disorders. Treatment involves lifelong restriction of phenylalanine in the diet and supplementation with tyrosine. With early detection and meticulous management, normal growth and intellectual functioning are possible.

OBESITY AND WEIGHT CONTROL

The World Health Organization has recognized obesity as a worldwide epidemic affecting more than 500 million adults and paradoxically coexisting with undernutrition in both developing and industrialized countries. There also have been reports of an alarming increase in childhood obesity worldwide. Obesity (excess body fat for stature) contributes to adverse health consequences such as high blood pressure, blood lipid abnormalities, coronary heart disease, congestive heart failure, ischemic stroke, type 2 diabetes, gallbladder disease, osteoarthritis, several common cancers (including colorectal, uterine, and postmenopausal breast cancers), and reduced life expectancy. Genes play a significant role in the regulation of body weight. Nevertheless, environmental factors such as calorie-rich diets and a sedentary lifestyle can be instrumental in determining how an individual's genetic heritage will unfold.

Dietary carbohydrates are not the problem in obesity. In some Asian cultures, for example, where carbohydrate foods such as rice are the predominant food, people are relatively thin and heart disease and diabetes rates are lower than they are in Western cultures. What matters in weight control is the ratio of food energy (calories) consumed to energy expended, over time.

Height-weight tables as a reference for healthy weights have been supplanted by the parameter known as the body mass index (BMI). The BMI estimates total body fat, although it is less sensitive than using a skinfold caliper or other method to measure body fat indirectly. The BMI is defined as weight in kilograms divided by the square of the height in metres: weight ÷ height2 = BMI. In 1997 the World Health Organization recommended international adoption of the definition of a healthy BMI for adult women and men as between 18.5 and 24.9. A BMI lower than 18.5 is considered underweight, while a BMI of 25 to 29.9 denotes overweight and 30 or higher indicates obesity. Definitions of overweight and obesity are more difficult to quantify for children, whose BMI changes with age.

A healthful eating plan for gradual weight loss in adults will likely contain about 1,200 to 1,500 kilocalories (kcal) per day, probably accompanied by a balanced vitamin and mineral supplement. A desirable weight loss is about one pound per week from fat stores (as opposed to lean tissue), which requires an energy deficit of 3,500 kcal, or about 500 kcal per day. Consuming less than 1,000 kcal per day is not recommended. A preferred approach would be to increase physical activity, which has the added benefit of helping to maintain lean tissue. Individuals who are severely obese and unable to lose weight may, after medical consultation, consider weight-loss medications that suppress appetite or decrease nutrient absorption or even surgery to reduce the volume of the stomach or bypass it altogether. Carbohydrate-restricted diets, very-low-fat diets, and novelty diets — those in which one food or food group is emphasized — may result in weight loss but generally fail to establish the good dietary and exercise practices necessary to maintain the desired weight, and weight is often regained shortly after the diet is stopped.

A successful approach to long-term weight management requires establishing new patterns: eating healthfully, but eating less; engaging in regular physical activity; and changing behaviour patterns that are counterproductive, such as eating while watching television. Limiting intake of fatty foods, which are more energy-rich, is also helpful, as is eating smaller portions and drinking water instead of calorie-containing drinks. Low-fat foods are not always low in total calories, as the fat may be replaced by sugars, which themselves provide calories. Individuals who use artificial or nonnutritive sweeteners do not necessarily reduce their total calorie intake.

Research with genetically obese laboratory animals led to the discovery of the *ob* gene in mice and humans. Under the direction of this gene, adipose (fat) tissue cells secrete leptin, a protein hormone. When fat stores increase, leptin sends a signal to the hypothalamus that stimulates one to eat less and expend more energy. Certain genetic mutations result in insufficient production of functional leptin or in a failure to respond to the leptin signal. Treatment with leptin may prove useful for the small percentage of obese persons who have a defect in the *ob* gene, although it is not yet known whether leptin therapy will induce weight loss in those who are leptin-resistant or who do not have mutations in the *ob* gene.

EATING DISORDERS

Eating disorders such as anorexia nervosa and bulimia nervosa are serious health problems reflecting an undue concern with body weight. Girls and young women are most vulnerable to the pressures of society to be thin, although boys and men can also fall prey to these disorders, which have lifelong consequences and can even be fatal. The incidence of eating disorders has risen during the last 50 years, particularly in the United States and western Europe.

Young athletes often restrict energy intakes to meet weight guidelines and body-image expectations of their sport. Females are most affected, but male athletes, such as gymnasts, wrestlers, boxers, and jockeys, are also vulnerable. Intense training among young female athletes, coupled with food energy restriction, often results in amenorrhea (failure to menstruate for at least three consecutive months) and bone loss similar to that at menopause. Calcium supplementation may be required.

ANOREXIA NERVOSA

Anorexia nervosa is an eating disorder characterized by the refusal of an emaciated individual to maintain a normal body weight. A person with anorexia nervosa typically weighs no more than 85 percent of the expected weight for the person's age, height, and sex, and in some cases much less. In addition, people with anorexia nervosa have a distorted evaluation of their own weight and body shape. They typically consider their emaciated bodies to be

A woman living with the effects of anorexia. There is a psychological component to anorexia, wherein the patient has a distorted image of his or her own body. Fred Dufour/AFP/ Getty Images

attractive or even a bit too fat, have a severely restricted and rigid diet, and have an intense fear of gaining weight. In women the weight loss is accompanied by amenorrhea, which means they stop menstruating. An estimated 5–20 percent of people with the disorder die as the result of starvation or medical complications that are caused by low weight and a restricted diet.

When the diagnosis of anorexia nervosa is given, a qualified health care professional also will determine whether the patient should also be diagnosed as having one of two types of illness: binge-eating/purging type or restricting type. The binge-eating/purging type is characterized by regular engagement in binge eating (eating of a significantly large amount of food during a given period of time) or purging (self-induced vomiting or misuse of laxatives, diuretics, or enemas) during the current episode of anorexia nervosa. The restricting type is characterized as unhealthy weight loss due to food restriction.

Although some people with anorexia nervosa also engage in binge eating followed by purging, in bulimia nervosa body weight generally remains near or above normal. Approximately 90 percent of all people diagnosed with anorexia nervosa are women, and most report onset of the illness between ages 12 and 25. An estimated 0.5–3.7 percent of women in the United States suffer from anorexia nervosa at some time in their life. However, partial-syndrome anorexia is far more common. Researchers report that close to 5 percent of adolescent girls have this "mild form" of anorexia nervosa, displaying some, but not all, of the clinical symptoms of the disorder.

British physician Sir Richard Morton is credited with the first English-language description of anorexia nervosa in 1689. He reported two adolescent cases, one female and one male, which he described as occurrences of "nervous consumption," a wasting away due to emotional turmoil.

In 1874 anorexia nervosa was introduced as a clinical diagnosis by two different physicians, Sir William Withey Gull of Britain and Charles Lasègue of France. Each emphasized varying aspects of the condition in their clinical reports, yet they both described anorexia as a "nervous" disease characterized by self-starvation. They were the first to recognize the illness as a distinct clinical diagnosis. When Gull reported about his work to the Clinical Society of London, he used the term "anorexia nervosa," which literally means "nervous loss of appetite," to describe the condition. He was the first to do so. Gull's reports were published by the society the following year, and the term later gained broad acceptance.

Cases of what is today recognized as anorexia nervosa have been documented throughout history, but it was not officially recognized as a psychiatric disorder until 1980, when its incidence increased greatly. Many experts blame the rise in anorexia nervosa on the unrelenting focus in the popular media on young women's appearance, especially the emphasis on thinness as an ideal. This emphasis is especially common in the cultural standards of beauty in affluent industrialized countries, and anorexia nervosa is far more prevalent in the United States, Europe, and industrialized Asia than it is elsewhere in the world.

Anorexia nervosa usually begins in adolescence or early adulthood. The causes of the illness are multifactorial and include genetic and biological risk factors, developmental factors that may contribute to a negative subjective body image, a lack of awareness of internal feelings (including hunger and emotions), a family history of eating disturbances, social influence, and psychological factors. Psychological factors can include a range of influences, such as an anxious temperament, perfectionistic or obsessive tendencies, a history of trauma, a co-occurring psychological disorder (e.g., depression, obsessive-compulsive disorder, attention deficit/hyperactivity disorder, and certain personality disorders), and either chronic or acute stress. A family history of alcohol or substance abuse; physical, emotional, or sexual abuse; mental illness; or high parental conflict also have been shown to increase risk. In addition, most cases of anorexia are preceded by an episode of dieting that progresses toward severe food restriction and self-starvation. However, it is not clear whether such dieting behaviour is a precursor to the illness or merely an early symptom.

Research has not identified a uniquely effective treatment for anorexia nervosa in adults. Various forms of psychotherapy and nutrition therapy are used in an attempt to treat it in such cases. For adolescent patients, family therapy that includes parents and sometimes siblings and a family-based treatment approach known as Maudsley therapy appear to be of benefit. Weight restoration is considered the key component to treatment, regardless of the age of onset, as studies show that many of the hallmark symptoms of anorexia are the result of starvation or semistarvation. Hospitalization may be required in cases of extreme weight loss because of its potentially life-threatening nature. People with anorexia nervosa typically are very rigid in their behaviours and are terrified of becoming fat, so the hospital's medical personnel sometimes may resort to coercive measures such as forced feeding or restricting privileges until there is a gain in weight. The disorder has proved to be challenging to treat with either psychotherapy or antidepressants. Ongoing research is investigating whether other psychotropic medications may be of use for recovery from anorexia. Studies show that about one-half of those who receive treatment for anorexia nervosa remain below their expected body weight even several years after treatment, and many of the rest continue to struggle with eating, dieting, and their body image.

BULIMIA NERVOSA

Bulimia nervosa, or simply bulimia, is an eating disorder characterized by binge eating followed by inappropriate attempts to compensate for the binge, such as self-induced vomiting or the excessive use of laxatives, diuretics, or enemas. In other cases, the binge eating is followed by excessive exercise or fasting. The episodes of binge eating and purging typically occur an average of twice a week or more over a period of at least three months, and repetition of the cycle can lead to serious medical complications such as dental decay or dehydration.

Individuals with bulimia nervosa, in contrast to anorexia nervosa, generally maintain a body weight near normal for their age, height, and sex. Both illnesses are accompanied by characteristic unhealthy weight-control methods and an intense fear of weight gain. Approximately 85–90 percent of the people diagnosed with bulimia nervosa are women. An estimated 1–3 percent of women in the United States suffer from bulimia nervosa at some time in their life. When the diagnostic criteria for bulimia nervosa are met, a qualified health care professional also will specify one of two types of the illness: purging type (episodes of binge eating are followed by self-induced vomiting or misuse of laxatives or enemas) or nonpurging type (episodes of binge eating are followed by fasting or excessive exercise).

Cases of binge eating followed by purging can be found in historical records, but bulimia nervosa was not officially recognized as a psychiatric disorder until 1980. The recognition of the diagnosis was due in large part to a dramatic increase in cases in the 1970s and '80s. Experts often attribute the increase to the intense focus in the popular media on thinness as an ideal for young women and to a greater recognition of the condition by health care professionals. The "thin ideal" referred to by experts is most prevalent in affluent industrialized countries, and it is in these countries that bulimia is most common.

Bulimia nervosa usually begins in adolescence or early adulthood. Some of the factors that appear to contribute to the development of the disorder are genetic and biological factors, chronic dieting, a lack of awareness of internal feelings (including hunger and emotions), a self-image that is unduly influenced by weight and body shape, a family history of eating disturbance or body image complaints, and a tendency toward self-judgment based on external standards rather than internal evaluations. Other emotional disorders, including depression, substance abuse disorders, and certain personality disorders, often coexist with bulimia nervosa, but it is not clear whether these disorders are precursors to the illness.

Cognitive behaviour therapy is the most widely researched and apparently the most effective treatment for bulimia nervosa. Treatment with cognitive behaviour therapy involves nutritional education, normalization of eating patterns, and addressing dysfunctional thought processes such as perfectionist thinking, especially concerning appearance or diet. Also useful in treating bulimia nervosa are antidepressant medications and interpersonal psychotherapy, a psychological technique that focuses on changing the way in which the patient relates to other people. These two alternatives, however, are generally considered to be secondary treatments because the benefits of antidepressant medications often last only as long as the medication continues to be taken, and interpersonal therapy produces beneficial results more slowly than cognitive behaviour therapy.

HEARTBURN AND PEPTIC ULCER

When gastric contents, containing hydrochloric acid, flow backward from the stomach, the lining of the esophagus becomes inflamed, leading to the burning sensation known as heartburn. Occasional heartburn (also known as acid indigestion) is a common occurrence, typically precipitated by eating certain foods. However, some people experience heartburn regularly, a condition known as gastroesophageal reflux disease (GERD). Individuals with GERD are advised to limit their intake of alcohol and caffeine, which relax the lower esophageal sphincter and actually promote reflux, as well as their intake of fat, which delays gastric emptying. Chocolate, citrus fruit and juices, tomatoes and tomato products, spearmint and peppermint oils, and certain spices may aggravate heartburn, but these foods do not appear to cause the condition.

For overweight or obese individuals with GERD, weight loss may have a beneficial effect on symptoms. Eating smaller meals, chewing food thoroughly, eating more slowly, avoiding tight-fitting clothes, not smoking, and not lying down before about three hours after eating are among the factors that may improve the condition. Without medical supervision, drugs such as antacids and acid controllers should be used only infrequently.

It is now known that a peptic ulcer (a sore on the lining of the stomach or duodenum) is not caused by stress or eating spicy foods, as was once thought. Rather, most peptic ulcers are caused by the infectious bacterial agent *Helicobacter pylori* and can be treated by a simple course of antibiotics. However, stress and dietary factors—such as coffee, other caffeinated beverages, and alcohol—can aggravate an existing ulcer.

BOWEL CONDITIONS AND DISEASES

Constipation, a condition characterized by the difficult passage of relatively dry, hardened feces, may arise from insufficient dietary fibre (roughage) or other dietary factors, such as taking calcium or iron supplements, in addition to daily routines that preclude relaxation. Straining during defecation can also contribute to diverticulosis, small outpouchings in the colonic wall, which may become inflamed (diverticulitis) and present serious complications. Another possible consequence of straining is hemorrhoids, swollen veins of the rectum and anus that typically lead to pain, itching, and bleeding. Constipation can usually be treated by eating high-fibre foods such as whole-grain breads and cereals, drinking sufficient amounts of water, and engaging in regular exercise. By drawing water into the large intestine (colon), fibre—especially the insoluble type—helps form a soft, bulky stool. Eating dried fruits such as prunes, which contain a natural laxative substance (dihydroxyphenyl isatin) as well as being high in fibre, also helps stimulate the bowels. Although laxatives or enemas may be helpful, frequent use may upset fluid, mineral, and electrolyte (salt) balances and interfere with vitamin absorption. Any persistent change in bowel habits should be evaluated by a physician.

In contrast to constipation, diarrhea—loose, watery stools, and possibly an increased frequency of bowel movements—can be a cause for immediate concern. Acute diarrhea of bacterial origin is relatively common and often self-limiting. Other common causes of acute diarrhea include viral infections, parasites, food intolerances or allergies, medications, medical or surgical treatments, and even stress. Regardless of cause, drinking fluids is important for treating a temporary bout of diarrhea. However, if severe and persisting, diarrhea can lead to potentially dangerous dehydration and electrolyte imbalances and requires urgent medical attention, especially in infants and children. Prolonged vomiting presents similar risks.

Inflammatory bowel disease (IBD), such as Crohn's disease (regional ileitis) or ulcerative colitis, results in impaired absorption of many nutrients, depending upon which portion of the gastrointestinal tract is affected. Children with IBD may fail to grow properly. Treatment generally includes a diet low in fat and fibre, high in protein and easily digestible carbohydrate, and free of lactose (milk sugar). Increased intakes of certain nutrients, such as iron, calcium, and magnesium, and supplementation with fat-soluble vitamins may also be recommended, along with additional fluid and electrolytes to replace losses due to diarrhea.

Irritable bowel syndrome (IBS) is a common gastrointestinal disorder characterized by a disturbance in intestinal peristalsis. Symptoms include excessive gas, abdominal discomfort, and cramps, as well as alternating diarrhea and constipation. Although it can be extremely uncomfortable, IBS does not cause intestinal damage. Dietary treatment involves identifying and avoiding "problem" foods, notably legumes and other gas-producing vegetables and dairy products, and possibly reducing caffeine consumption. For most people with IBS, a low-fat diet, smaller meals, and a gradual increase in fibre intake are helpful.

TOOTH DECAY

Dental caries (tooth decay) is an oral infectious disease in which bacteria, primarily *Streptococcus mutans*, in the dental plaque metabolize simple sugars and other fermentable carbohydrates into acids that dissolve tooth

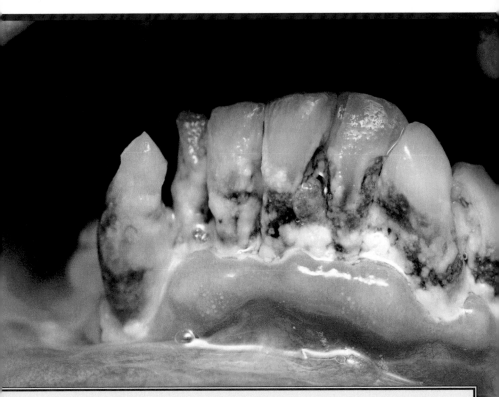

Teeth showing the ravages of decay. Fermentable carbohydrates such as sugar can coat teeth with plaque and bacteria, which destroy protective enamel and cause teeth to rot. Koshy Johnson/Oxford Scientific/Getty Images

enamel. Dental plaque (not to be confused with the lipid-containing plaque found in arteries) is a mass of bacteria and sticky polymers that shield the tooth from saliva and the tongue, thereby facilitating decay.

All dietary forms of sugar, including honey, molasses, brown sugar, and corn syrup, can cause tooth decay. Fermentable carbohydrates in crackers, breads, cereals, and other grain products, as well as milk, fruits, and fruit juices, also have cariogenic (decay-causing) potential. Eating sugary or starchy foods between meals, especially sticky foods that stay on the teeth longer, increases the time that teeth are exposed to destructive acids. Artificial sweeteners are not cariogenic, and xylitol, a sugar alcohol used in some chewing gums, is even cariostatic, meaning that it reduces new tooth decay by inhibiting plaque and suppressing decay-causing bacteria. Putting an infant to sleep with a bottle, especially one containing juice or other sweetened beverages, milk, or infant formula can lead to a condition called "baby bottle tooth decay."

Fluoride is extremely effective at protecting tooth enamel from decay, especially while enamel is being formed in the jaws before the permanent teeth erupt. Fluoridation of water in communities where fluoride is not naturally high is a safe and effective public health measure. Water with approximately one part per million of fluoride protects against dental caries without causing the mottling of teeth that can occur at higher levels. In areas without fluoridated water, fluoride supplements are recommended for children. Brewed tea, marine fish consumed with bones, and seaweed are significant food sources of fluoride.

Regular brushing and flossing of the teeth and gums, as well as rinsing the mouth after meals and snacks, are important measures that protect against periodontal (gum) disease as well as dental caries. Gum health also depends on a properly functioning immune system and good overall nutrition. Key nutrients include vitamin C, which helps protect against gingivitis (inflamed gums), and calcium and vitamin D, which help ensure a strong jawbone and teeth.

CHAPTER 9

FOOD AND ENVIRONMENTAL FACTORS

In addition to supplying the body with energy, food is capable of producing other effects upon ingestion. Among these are food-drug interactions and food allergies, such as immunological reactions to peanuts and shellfish. Food is also susceptible to contamination, such as with agricultural chemicals (e.g., pesticides) or industrial chemicals (e.g., dioxins) or with infectious agents, which underlie outbreaks of foodborne illness. The interactions between food and environmental factors can have significant impacts on human health, regardless of their origins.

FOOD-DRUG INTERACTIONS

Drugs may interfere with or enhance the utilization of nutrients, sometimes leading to imbalances. A common example is the increased loss of potassium that results from the use of certain diuretics to treat high blood pressure. Nutrient absorption can also be affected by drugs that change the acidity of the gastrointestinal tract, alter digestive function, or actually bind to nutrients. For example, regular use of laxatives, antacids, or mineral oil can reduce nutrient absorption and over time may lead to deficiency. Elderly individuals who take multiple medicines are particularly at risk of impaired nutritional status.

On the other hand, foods can alter drug absorption or interact with drugs in undesirable ways, resulting in drug ineffectiveness or toxicity. For example, protein and vitamin B_6 interfere with the effectiveness of levodopa, used to treat Parkinson's disease. Tyramine, an amino-acid derivative found in certain aged cheeses and red wines, may cause hypertension in individuals being treated for depression with monoamine oxidase (MAO) inhibitors. Grapefruit juice contains unique substances that can block the breakdown of some drugs, thereby affecting their absorption and effectiveness. These drugs include certain cholesterol-lowering statins, calcium channel blockers, anticonvulsant agents, estrogen, antihistamines, protease inhibitors, immunosuppressants, antifungal drugs, and psychiatric medications. Eating grapefruit or drinking grapefruit juice within a few hours or even a few days of taking these medications could result in unintended consequences.

Vitamin and mineral supplements and herbal products can also interact with medicines. For example, one or more of the supplemental antioxidants studied—vitamin C, vitamin E, beta-carotene, and selenium—may blunt the effectiveness of certain drugs (e.g., high-dose niacin, when used in combination with statins) in raising HDL cholesterol levels and improving cardiovascular health. Also, the herbal supplement St. John's wort can alter the metabolism of drugs such as protease inhibitors, anticlotting drugs, and antidepressants, and it can reduce the effectiveness of oral contraceptives.

FOOD ALLERGIES AND INTOLERANCES

A true food allergy involves an abnormal immunologic response to an otherwise harmless food component, usually a protein. In the case of antibody-mediated (immediate hypersensitivity) food allergies, within minutes or hours of exposure to the allergen, the body produces specific immunoglobulin E antibodies and releases chemical mediators such as histamine, resulting in gastrointestinal, skin, or respiratory symptoms ranging from mild to life-threatening. Much less common are cell-mediated (delayed hypersensitivity) food allergies, in which a localized inflammatory process and other symptoms may not start for up to a day. Adverse food reactions that do not involve the immune system, aside from foodborne infection or poisoning, are called food intolerances or sensitivities. Most common of these is lactose intolerance, which is a genetically determined deficiency of the enzyme lactase that is needed to digest the milk sugar, lactose.

Milk allergy and lactose intolerance are distinct conditions that are often confused. Only about 1 percent of the population has a true allergy to the protein in cow's milk. Milk allergy is found most often in infants, whose immune and digestive systems are immature. On the other hand, much of the world's population, except those of northern European descent, is to some degree lactose intolerant after early childhood. Undigested lactose reaching the large intestine can cause abdominal discomfort, flatulence, and diarrhea. Lactose-intolerant individuals can often handle with little or no discomfort small quantities of dairy products, especially yogurt or other milk products containing the bacterium *Lactobacillus acidophilus*. Alternatives are the use of lactose-hydrolyzed milk products or lactase tablets or drops, which convert lactose to simple, digestible sugars.

Celiac disease (also known as celiac sprue, nontropical sprue, or gluten-sensitive enteropathy) is a hereditary disorder in which consumption of wheat gluten and related proteins from rye and barley is not tolerated. Recent studies indicate that oats may be safe if not contaminated with wheat. Celiac disease, which may be a type of cell-mediated food allergy, affects primarily individuals of European descent and rarely those of African or Asian descent. It is characterized by inflammatory damage to the mucosal cells lining the small intestine, leading to malabsorption of nutrients and such symptoms as diarrhea, fatigue, weight loss, bone pain, and neurological disturbances. Multiple nutritional deficiencies may ensue and, in children, growth is impaired. The disorder is often associated with autoimmune conditions, particularly autoimmune thyroid disease and type 1 diabetes. Although celiac disease can be life-threatening if untreated, patients can recover if gluten is eliminated from the diet.

A logo signifying that a product does not contain gluten. People with celiac disease must maintain a gluten-free diet to control their symptoms, which include diarrhea, pain, and fatigue. © Shutterstock.com/AGCuesta

Other adverse reactions to foods or beverages may be drug effects, such as those caused by caffeine or alcohol. Certain foods, such as ripened cheese, chocolate, red wine, and even ice cream, trigger headaches in some individuals. Food additives that can cause reactions in susceptible people include sulfite preservatives, used in some wines, dried fruits, and dried potato products; nitrate and nitrite preservatives, used in processed meats; certain food colorants, particularly tartrazine (also known as FD&C Yellow #5); and the flavour enhancer monosodium glutamate (MSG). Some adverse reactions to food are purely psychological and do not occur when the food is served in a disguised form.

Nearly any food has allergenic potential, but foods that most commonly cause antibody-mediated allergic reactions are cow's milk, eggs, wheat, fish, shellfish, soybeans, peanuts, and tree nuts (such as almonds, walnuts, and cashews). Depending on processing methods, edible oils and other products derived from these foods may still contain allergenic protein residues. Severely allergic people may react to extremely small amounts of an offending food, even inhaled vapours.

Studies differ significantly as to the percentage of adults and children who have true food allergies. However, all seem to agree that few adults (about 2 to 5 percent) and slightly more children (up to 7 or 8 percent) are affected. Most children outgrow food allergies, particularly if the offending food is avoided for a year or two. However, food allergies can develop at any time, and some allergies, such as those to peanuts, tree nuts, and shellfish, may be lifelong. Common symptoms of antibody-mediated food allergy include tightening of the throat, swelling of the lips or tongue, itchy lips, wheezing, difficulty breathing, headache, nasal congestion, skin rash (eczema), hives, nausea, vomiting, stomach cramps, diarrhea and, in severe cases, life-threatening anaphylactic shock. People susceptible to anaphylaxis are advised to carry a syringe loaded with epinephrine at all times and to seek emergency medical care if an allergic reaction begins.

Food allergies are often hard to document, even by physicians trained in allergy and immunology. Blood tests for antibodies to specific allergens, skin tests, and even an elimination diet, in which suspect foods are eliminated from the diet and then added back one at a time, may not be definitive. The most conclusive diagnostic test is a so-called double-blind food challenge, in which neither doctor nor patient knows whether a suspect food or a harmless placebo is being given. However, these controlled clinical tests are expensive and time-consuming.

Labels are important for identifying hidden ingredients in packaged foods, although they are often imprecise and cannot be relied on naively. For example, even if a product is labeled as nondairy, a listing of casein, caseinate, or whey indicates the presence of milk protein. Peanuts may be found in unlikely foods, such as chili, stew, processed meats, oils, flours, cream substitutes, and desserts.

TOXINS IN FOODS

Edible skins of fruits and vegetables are rich in vitamins, minerals, and fibre. However, pesticide residues and other environmental contaminants are typically more plentiful in the outer layers of these foods. Pesticides also tend to accumulate in the fat and skin of animals. Intake of toxic substances is reduced by consuming a wide variety of foods; washing fruits and vegetables carefully; and trimming fat from meat and poultry and removing skin from poultry and fish. Even organic produce requires thorough washing: it may not have synthetic chemicals, but mold, rot, fecal matter, or other natural substances can contaminate it at any point from field to market. Peeling helps reduce these unwanted chemicals and microbes, although valuable nutrients will be lost as well.

A greenish tinge on potatoes, although merely the harmless substance chlorophyll, indicates that the natural toxicant solanine may be present. Solanine builds up when a potato is handled roughly, exposed to light or extremes

A chef washing produce before preparing a meal. Washing helps rid food of pesticides and environmental toxins that can be harmful if consumed. © iStockphoto.com/gerenme

of temperature, or is old. Symptoms of solanine poisoning include diarrhea, cramps, and headache, although many damaged potatoes would have to be eaten to cause serious illness. Peeling away green areas or removing sprouts or the entire skin (despite its high nutrient content) reduces solanine intake.

Swordfish and shark, as well as tuna steaks, may contain high levels of methylmercury (which remains after cooking) and should be avoided by pregnant women. Nonbacterial toxins in seafood include scombrotoxin (histamine) in spoiled fish, which can result in a severe allergic reaction when eaten; dinoflagellates (microscopic algae), associated with the so-called red tide, which can cause paralytic shellfish poisoning when consumed; and ciguatera, found in certain warm-water reef fish.

Natural toxins in some species of mushrooms cause symptoms ranging from gastrointestinal upset to neurological effects, even hallucinations. Most mushroom fatalities are due to consumption of amatoxins in *Amanita phalloides*, the mushroom species known as the death cap, which, if not lethal, can cause lasting liver and kidney damage. As there are no antidotes for mushroom poisoning, and identification of mushroom species by inexperienced mushroom pickers is often imprecise, consumption of wild mushrooms is not advised.

CHEMICALS AND FOOD SAFETY

Threats to food safety pose major risks to human health, and hence the production, processing, and handling of food is of significant concern to national governments and international health organizations. In the early 21st century, however, information about food contamination with the chemicals acrylamide and melamine pushed food safety to the forefront of public attention.

ACRYLAMIDE TOXICITY

Acrylamide is a white, odourless, crystalline organic compound that is produced as a result of industrial processes and that is generated in certain foods as a result of cooking at high temperatures. In the 1950s and '60s, it was identified as a potential source of occupational neurotoxicity in persons involved in its industrial manufacture. The chemical can enter the body via inhalation of contaminated air, absorption through the skin, and consumption of contaminated food or water. Although the body is capable of metabolizing acrylamide, leading to its excretion in the urine, acute toxicity can cause confusion, muscle weakness, loss of coordination, and hallucination. Contact with the skin can cause irritation.

In rodents, chronic low-level exposure to acrylamide is associated with adverse effects on reproductive health and with the development of cancer. In 1994, based on information from rodent studies, the International Agency for Research on Cancer (IARC) listed acrylamide as a probable carcinogen in humans. (Probable carcinogens are designated Group 2A by the IARC; Group 1 contains compounds known to be carcinogenic in humans, whereas Group 2A compounds are probably carcinogenic and Group 2B compounds are possibly carcinogenic.)

In 1997 an investigation of cattle and fish that died from paralysis in southwestern Sweden linked the use of copious amounts of acrylamide in a tunnel-construction project in the region to the contamination of local groundwater and surface water. Some of the tunnel workers experienced low levels of neurotoxicity. Because of the incident, Swedish researchers initiated a new series of investigations to determine the extent to which acrylamide is toxic in humans. In 2002, during the course of these investigations, scientists working at Stockholm

University in Sweden discovered acrylamide in cooked carbohydrate-rich foods.

The ubiquity of acrylamide in processed food has complicated studies of its potential cancer-causing effects in humans. As a result, epidemiological research attempting to confirm suggested associations between acrylamide and increased risk for certain types of cancer have been inconclusive. Because acrylamide is recognized as a probable carcinogen, however, some cereal and potato-chip manufacturers have made efforts to reduce the amount of acrylamide in their products.

MISUSE OF MELAMINE

Melamine is a crystalline organic compound that is used as a starting material for the manufacture of synthetic resins. The misuse of melamine, namely the adulteration of various food products with the chemical, raised significant public health and food safety concerns in the first decade of the 21st century. Beginning in the late 1950s, melamine was utilized as a nonprotein nitrogen (NPN) compound in ruminant feed, since microorganisms in the ruminant stomach are able to metabolize the chemical into protein. However, the addition of melamine to animal feeds was later discouraged, since the process of microbial protein generation from melamine was inefficient and resulted in the release of potentially toxic amounts of ammonia by-product. Although many manufacturers switched to the use of more-efficiently metabolized NPNs such as urea, melamine use in animal feeds persisted, particularly in China, where manufacturers illegally added large amounts of melamine to a variety of products to pass industry tests, specifically the Dumas test and the Kjeldahl method. These tests are frequently used to detect protein levels in milk and other food products based on nitrogen content.

Because melamine is abundant in nitrogen, these tests are unable to distinguish between melamine-contaminated and melamine-free products.

Evidence of misuse of the chemical in China emerged in 2007, when more than 4,000 dogs and cats in the United States died from kidney failure as a result of ingesting melamine-tainted pet food. The substance was found in wheat gluten and in rice protein concentrate that had been imported from China and used in the United States to make the foods. Some 100 brands of pet foods were recalled as a result of the incident. The following year, melamine contamination of infant formula in China led to the hospitalization of more than 50,000 infants as a result of renal dysfunction. Studies of melamine toxicity in humans and pets revealed that, although low-level exposure to the chemical does not usually cause adverse health affects, in high concentrations it crystallizes in the urine, leading to kidney stones and other renal disorders. An investigation into the contamination of infant formula conducted within China in 2008 traced the production of tainted products to more than 20 dairy manufacturers. Chinese dairy product exports, including certain chocolate and milk products, were also found to contain melamine and were subsequently recalled in Australia, New Zealand, Hong Kong, Singapore, and Thailand.

Melamine-based plastics sold as dinnerware and kitchenware have also raised safety concerns. Melamine plastics degrade and release chemical constituents upon heating to temperatures utilized for cooking in ovens and microwaves, as well as upon exposure to acidic foodstuffs. As a result, there is a risk of melamine and formaldehyde discharge into foods prepared or stored in melamine-containing dishes, bowls, and other products in the home. Although the extent of impact on human health from chemical degradation due to heating remains unclear, manufacturers of melamine plastics typically supply instructions on the safe use of their products in order to minimize risk. Advancements in heat-stability of melamine-based plastics have also helped reduce the risk of chemical leaching.

FOODBORNE ILLNESSES

Contamination of foods or beverages with disease-causing organisms—bacteria, viruses, fungi, and parasites—can result in symptoms ranging from mild stomach upset, headache, muscle aches, and fever to abdominal cramps, vomiting, and diarrhea. Severe cases can result in dangerous dehydration, nerve damage, paralysis, kidney failure, and death. Symptoms may develop within hours or days after eating contaminated food, and they are not always easy to distinguish from influenza or other illnesses. Drinking clear liquids (such as chicken broth, juices, and water) helps replace fluids and electrolytes lost during a mild infection, but immediate medical attention is required when symptoms are severe. Most susceptible are infants and young children, pregnant women, the elderly, and people with weakened immune systems or certain chronic diseases. Particularly risky foods include raw or undercooked meat, poultry, eggs, seafood, and unpasteurized (raw) milk products and juices.

Most cases of foodborne illness are caused by bacteria and the toxins they produce. *Campylobacter jejuni*, found in raw or undercooked foods of animal origin, especially poultry, is responsible for more diarrheal illness throughout the world than any other bacterium. Travelers' diarrhea is often caused by specific types of *Escherichia coli* bacteria, while other *E. coli* types cause much of the diarrhea in infants, particularly during weaning, in developing countries. Other common foodborne infections are caused

GERMAN *E. COLI* OUTBREAK OF 2011

By July 2011, an outbreak of *E. coli* that began in April in the northern region of Germany had become the deadliest and the second largest *E. coli* outbreak on record. It was responsible for a total of 4,321 cases and 50 deaths, most of which occurred in and around Hamburg in northern Germany. The minority of cases and deaths reported outside Germany, in places such as Denmark, Sweden, the Netherlands, and the United Kingdom, occurred in persons who had visited the country just prior to their illness. (The largest outbreak was in Japan in 1996, in which more than 12,600 people became infected.)

Investigators were led to bean sprouts produced at a farm in northern Germany, just south of Hamburg. Growing sprouts require warm, humid conditions, and such conditions also support the growth of various types of bacteria. Hence, sprouts often are associated with outbreaks of foodborne illness. French health officials reported a small number of HUS cases linked to Shiga toxin-producing *E. coli* near Bordeaux, where eight people were hospitalized after consuming arugula, fenugreek, and mustard sprouts. The same strain of *E. coli* was at fault for the outbreak.

A task force set up by the European Food and Safety Authority tracked the source to a single lot of fenugreek seeds imported from Egypt by a German distributor in November 2009. The distributor sold the seeds to about 70 companies, more than 50 of which were in Germany. The task force believed it was likely that this single lot of sprouts was the common link between the French and German outbreaks but also cautioned that other lots may have been contaminated as well. Consumers were discouraged from growing sprouts for consumption and were advised to avoid eating raw sprouts. Suspected Egyptian seeds were pulled from the European market, and the import of fenugreek seeds into Europe from Egypt was temporarily banned.

by various strains of *Salmonella* bacteria and the Norwalk family of viruses.

Smoking, drying, fermenting, and the adding of sugar or salt are traditional methods used to preserve food and keep it safe. During the 20th century public health advances such as disinfection of water supplies, pasteurization of milk, safe canning, widespread use of refrigeration, and improved food-safety practices eliminated typhoid fever, tuberculosis, and cholera, for example, as common foodborne diseases. However, others have taken their place. New causes of foodborne illness continue to be discovered or described. A recently characterized microscopic parasite, *Cyclospora cayetanensis*, was the cause of outbreaks of diarrheal illness in the United States and Canada starting in 1996. Guatemalan raspberries, contaminated with *Cyclospora* via the water supply, were the suspected source of infection. Another recently described parasite, *Cryptosporidium parvum*, contaminates water supplies and foods and is an important cause of diarrhea throughout the world, particularly in children and in persons with HIV.

In 1993, undercooked hamburgers emerged in the United States as a potential source of *E. coli* O157:H7, a deadly strain of a normally harmless bacterium found in the human digestive tract. Subsequently, this microbe has also been found in unpasteurized fruit juice, such as fresh-pressed apple cider, and other foods possibly contaminated with animal feces. The bacterium produces a potent toxin that may result in bloody diarrhea. Hemolytic uremic syndrome, a possible complication, is a major cause of acute kidney failure in children. *E. coli* O157:H7 infection, which can be spread by persons who unknowingly incubate the bacterium in their intestines and transmit it through poor toilet hygiene, appears to be on the rise worldwide, particularly in North America and western Europe.

Certain other bacteria also produce a toxin, which then causes a poisoning or intoxication rather than a bacterial infection per se. For example, *Clostridium botulinum*, found in improperly canned foods, produces the lethal neurotoxin that causes botulism. The toxin responsible for staphylococcal food poisoning is produced by *Staphylococcus aureus* typically after contamination from nasal passages or cuts on the skin.

Many molds (fungi) on food are harmless and, in fact, are flavour enhancing, such as those used to ripen certain cheeses. However, some molds—particularly those on grains, nuts, fruits, and seeds—produce poisons known as mycotoxins. The mycotoxins of greatest concern are aflatoxins, which can infect nuts, peanuts, corn, and wheat. Prolonged low-level exposure to aflatoxins, as seen in regions of Asia and Africa, is suspected of contributing to liver cancer. Discarding nuts that are discoloured, shriveled, or moldy helps reduce the risk.

Eating raw shellfish, sushi, or undercooked fish puts one at risk for parasites, such as tapeworms, as well as for bacteria and viruses, all of which are killed by proper cooking. The great majority of seafood-related illness is caused by the consumption of raw bivalve mollusks. Clams, mussels, and scallops, which are usually served cooked, are of less public health concern than oysters, which are often eaten raw.

Bovine spongiform encephalopathy (BSE), commonly known as mad cow disease, was first seen in British cattle in the 1980s. However, it was not linked to human disease until 1996, when 10 young adults in the United Kingdom died of variant Creutzfeldt-Jakob disease, a fatal brain-wasting disease thought to have been transmitted by consumption of meat containing brain or spinal tissue from BSE-infected cattle. It is suspected that the diseased cattle had been infected by eating the ground remains of sheep with the neurodegenerative disease scrapie. BSE appears to be caused by infectious protein particles called prions, which kill brain cells and leave holes in the brain. Details of disease transmission are still unclear, as is the potential risk from cosmetics, dietary supplements, gelatin, or vaccines containing bovine ingredients, or from blood transfusions. Ground beef, sausages, and frankfurters are more likely to be contaminated with nervous-system tissue than are whole cuts of beef. Dairy products are considered safe, even if they come from BSE-infected cows.

Good personal hygiene and food safety practices are important in protecting against foodborne illness. The main source of contamination is fecal matter, which is reduced by frequently washing hands with soap and hot water, especially before preparing food. Thorough washing also decontaminates towels, surfaces, cutting boards, utensils, and other equipment that has touched uncooked meat. Other food safety guidelines include keeping cold foods cold, keeping hot foods hot, and refrigerating leftovers quickly.

Growth of microorganisms, parasites, and insects on certain foods (such as meat, poultry, spices, fruits, and vegetables) can be controlled by low-dose irradiation, which has been approved for specific uses in a number of countries, such as Japan, France, Italy, Mexico, and the United States. Food irradiation technology—which does not make foods radioactive—is considered safe by the World Health Organization and various health agencies, but it has yet to receive wide consumer acceptance.

CONCLUSION

Nutrition is of universal importance to human health. Hence, achieving an improved knowledge of the fundamental facets of human nutrition, from identifying the effects of nutrients on cellular processes to understanding the role of nutrients in the prevention and treatment of disease, is considered a key goal of scientific research. Such work could shed new light on food allergies or food-drug interactions and lead to the development of new therapeutic agents, such as antioxidants for certain types of cancer.

Beyond the realm of basic science, governments and health officials are working to address issues such as the need for greater nutritional education and access to educational resources. The importance of these issues has been emphasized by the increasing prevalence of nutrition-related disorders, such as obesity and diabetes, in countries worldwide, including those that are less-developed and suffer from inadequate health care infrastructure. In the early 21st century, the problem of obesity, particularly among low-income populations, fueled investigations into the relationship between socioeconomic factors and healthy diet. Among the areas of intense interest today are food deserts, which are impoverished areas where residents lack access to healthy foods. Food deserts may exist in rural or urban areas and are associated with complex geographic, economic, political, and social factors that, in turn, influence residents' diet and health.

Some countries where food deserts have been determined to exist have introduced measures to improve access to healthy foods. These measures include finding ways to promote the establishment of healthy food retailers in these areas and to connect consumers to outlets where fresh vegetables and fruits and other healthy foods are available at reasonable cost. The latter may be accomplished through farmers' markets, exposure to healthy foods in schools, urban garden and agriculture projects, or even online supermarkets that offer healthy foods for order over the Internet and delivery to accessible locations.

APPENDIX: TABLES

THE VITAMINS

TAMIN	ALTERNATIVE NAMES/FORMS	BIOLOGICAL FUNCTION	SYMPTOMS OF DEFICIENCY
WATER-SOLUBLE			
iamin	Vitamin B_1	Component of a coenzyme in carbohydrate metabolism; supports normal nerve function	Impairment of the nerves and heart muscle wasting
oflavin	Vitamin B_2	Component of coenzymes required for energy production and lipid, vitamin, mineral, and drug metabolism; antioxidant	Inflammation of the skin, tongue, and lips; ocular disturbances; nervous symptoms
iacin	Nicotinic acid, nicotinamide	Component of coenzymes used broadly in cellular metabolism, oxidation of fuel molecules, and fatty acid and steroid synthesis	Skin lesions, gastrointestinal disturbances, nervous symptoms
min B_6	Pyridoxine, pyridoxal, pyridoxamine	Component of coenzymes in metabolism of amino acids and other nitrogen-containing compounds; synthesis of hemoglobin, neurotransmitters; regulation of blood glucose levels	Dermatitis, mental depression, confusion, convulsions, anemia

THE VITAMINS

VITAMIN	ALTERNATIVE NAMES/FORMS	BIOLOGICAL FUNCTION	SYMPTOMS OF DEFICIENCY
WATER-SOLUBLE			
Folic acid	Folate, folacin, pteroylglutamic acid	Component of coenzymes in DNA synthesis, metabolism of amino acids; required for cell division, maturation of red blood cells	Impaired formation of red blood cells, weakness, irritability, headache, palpitations, inflammation of mouth, neural tube defects in fetus
Vitamin B_{12}	Cobalamin, cyanocobalamin	Cofactor for enzymes in metabolism of amino acids (including folic acid) and fatty acids; required for new cell synthesis, normal blood formation, and neurological function	Smoothness of the tongue, gastrointestinal disturbance, nervous symptoms
Pantothenic acid		As component of coenzyme A, essential for metabolism of carbohydrate, protein, and fat; cofactor for elongation of fatty acids	Weakness, gastrointestinal disturbance, nervous symptoms, fatigue, sleep disturbances, restlessness, nausea
Biotin		Cofactor in carbohydrate, fatty acid, and amino acid metabolism	Dermatitis, hair loss, conjunctivitis, neurological symptoms

THE VITAMINS

ITAMIN	ALTERNATIVE NAMES/FORMS	BIOLOGICAL FUNCTION	SYMPTOMS OF DEFICIENCY
WATER-SOLUBLE			
tamin C	Ascorbic acid	Antioxidant; synthesis of collagen, carnitine, amino acids, and hormones; immune function; enhances absorption of non-heme iron (from plant foods)	Swollen and bleeding gums, soreness and stiffness of the joints and lower extremities, bleeding under the skin and in deep tissues, slow wound healing, anemia

THE VITAMINS

TAMIN	ALTERNATIVE NAMES/FORMS	BIOLOGICAL FUNCTION	SYMPTOMS OF DEFICIENCY
FAT-SOLUBLE			
amin A	Retinol, retinal, retinoic acid, beta-carotene (plant version)	Normal vision, integrity of epithelial cells (mucous membranes and skin), reproduction, embryonic development, growth, immune response	Ocular disturbances leading to blindness, growth retardation, dry skin, diarrhea, vulnerability to infection
amin D	Calciferol, calatriol (1,25-dihydroxy vitamin D1 or vitamin D hormone), cholecalciferol (D3; plant version), ergocalciferol (D2; animal version)	Maintenance of blood calcium and phosphorus levels, proper mineralization of bones	Defective bone growth in children, soft bones in adults

THE VITAMINS

VITAMIN	ALTERNATIVE NAMES/FORMS	BIOLOGICAL FUNCTION	SYMPTOMS O DEFICIENCY
FAT-SOLUBLE			
Vitamin E	Alpha-tocopherol, tocopherol, tocotrienol	Antioxidant; interruption of free radical chain reactions; protection of polyunsaturated fatty acids, cell membranes	Peripheral neuropathy, breakdown of blood cells
Vitamin K	Phylloquinone, menaquinone, menadione, naphthoquinone	Synthesis of proteins involved in blood coagulation and bone metabolism	Impaired clotti of the blood a internal bleedi

COMPARING APPLES AND ORANGES: A NUTRIENT SCORECARD

FRUIT	NUTRIENT INDEX (DAILY VALUE PER 100 GRAMS [3.2 OUNCES])	CALORIES PER NUTRI
Kiwi	16	03.8
Papaya	14	02.8
Cantaloupe	13	05.9
Strawberries	12	02.5
Mango	11	04.2
Lemon	11	05.7
Orange (Florida)	11	05.1
Red Currents	10	05.7
Mandarin orange	09	05.1

COMPARING APPLES AND ORANGES: A NUTRIENT SCORECARD

FRUIT	NUTRIENT INDEX (DAILY VALUE PER 100 GRAMS [3.2 OUNCES])	CALORIES PER NUTRIENT
Avocado	08	20.9
Tangarine	08	05.2
Grapefruit	07	04.3
Lime	07	04.3
Apricot	07	07.3
Raspberries	07	06.4
Honeydew melon	06	06.0
Pinapple	05	10.2
Persimmon	05	14.6
Grapes (empress)	04	17.9
Blueberries	04	14.0
Plum	04	13.4
Banana	04	22.4
Watermelon	03	09.4
Peach	03	13.4
Nectarine	03	15.3
Cherries	03	21.0
Pear	02	32.8
Apple (with peel)	02	32.8

Source: Paul A. Lachance and A. Elizabeth Sloan, "A Nutritional Assessment of Major Fruits."

COMMON FOODBORNE ILLNESSES

ILLNESS (AND CAUSATIVE ORGANISM)	COMMON FOOD SOURCES	SYMPTOMS	SYMPTOM ONSET
ILLNESSES CAUSED BY BACTERIA			
Botulism (*Clostridium botulinum*)	Canned foods, honey (for infants)	Nausea, vomiting, headache, dizziness, difficulty swallowing and speaking, muscle weakness and paralysis, fatigue, blurred or double vision	18-36 hou
Campylobacteriosis (*Campylobacter jejuni*)	Raw or undercooked chicken, unpasteurized milk, non-chlorinated water	Watery or bloody diarrhea, vomiting, fever, nausea, muscle pain, abdominal cramps	2-5 day
Cholera (*Vibrio cholerae*)	Shellfish, contaminated water	Abdominal cramps, diarrhea, vomiting, dehydration, coma, cardiovascular collapse	6 hours-days
E. coli infection (*Escherichia coli*, O157:H7, and other strains)	Undercooked beef (especially ground), unpasteurized milk and fruit juices, dry-cured salami, alfalfa sprouts, contaminated water, raw fruits and vegetables	Watery or bloody diarrhea, abdominal cramps, acute kidney failure	12-72 hou
Listeriosis (*Listeria monocytogenes*)	Unpasteurized milk, soft cheeses	Fever, nausea, vomiting, diarrhea, encephalitis, blood infection, miscarriage or stillbirth in pregnant women, headache	Gastrointe inal symp toms, mo than 12 hours; seri symptoms days-3 we

COMMON FOODBORNEILLNESSES

LNESS (AND CAUSATIVE ORGANISM)	COMMON FOOD SOURCES	SYMPTOMS	SYMPTOM ONSET
ILLNESSES CAUSED BY BACTERIA			
fringens food poisoning Clostridium erfringens)	Improperly cooked or stored meat products	Diarrhea, abdominal cramps	8-24 hours
almonellosis nontyphoid Salmonella species)	Raw or under-cooked eggs, poultry, meat, or fish; unpasteurized milk	Nausea, abdominal cramps, diarrhea, fever, chills, vomiting, headache	6-48 hours
Shigellosis (Shigella)	Salads (potato, shrimp, macaroni, chicken), raw vegetables, dairy products, poultry, contaminated water	Watery or bloody diarrhea, abdominal cramps, vomiting	5-50 hours
aphylococcal od poisoning aphylococcus aureus)	Meat, eggs, poultry, tuna, potato and macaroni salads, cream-filled pastries	Nausea, vomiting, abdominal cramps, headache, muscle cramping, fatigue	2-6 hours
Typhoid Salmonella typhi)	Sewage-contaminated water, shellfish, raw fruits and vegetables, dairy products	Fever, chills, headache, abdominal pain, constipation, enlarged spleen, rash, intestinal perforation or hemorrhage	1-3 weeks

COMMON FOODBORNE ILLNESSES

ILLNESS (AND CAUSATIVE ORGANISM)	COMMON FOOD SOURCES	SYMPTOMS	SYMPT ONSE
ILLNESSES CAUSED BY BACTERIA			
Vibriosis (Vibrio parahaemolyticus and Vibrio vulnificus)	Raw, undercooked, or recontaminated seafood	Gastroenteritis, bloody or watery diarrhea, fever, blood infection, abdominal pain, chills, weakness	4-9(hour
Versiniosis (Yersinia enterocolitica)	Raw vegetables and meat, water, unpasteurized milk	Fever, abdominal pain, diarrhea, vomiting, headache, nausea, malaise	24-4 hour

COMMON FOODBORNE ILLNESSES

ILLNESS (AND CAUSATIVE ORGANISM)	COMMON FOOD SOURCES	SYMPTOMS	SYMPT ONSE
ILLNESSES CAUSED BY VIRUSES			
Hepatitis A (hepatitis A virus)	Contaminated water, shellfish, salads	Fever, malaise, nausea, anorexia, abdominal discomfort, jaundice	10-5 days
Norwalk-like virus	Shellfish, contaminated water, salad ingredients	Vomiting, diarrhea, nausea, abdominal pain	24-4 hour

NESS (AND CAUS- IVE ORGANISM)	COMMON FOOD SOURCES	SYMPTOMS	SYMPTOM ONSET
ILLNESSES CAUSED BY PARASITIC PROTOZOANS AND WORMS			
Amebiasis (Entamoeba histolytica)	Contaminated water, raw fruits or vegetables, unpasteurized dairy products	Gastrointestinal distress, bloody diarrhea, abdomi- nal cramps, intestinal ulcers	4-96 hours
yptosporidiosis ryptosporidium parvum)	Contaminated water, raw fruits and vegetables	Diarrhea, abdomi- nal cramps, fever	24-48 hours
yclosporiasis (Cyclospora cayetanensis)	Contaminated water, Guatemalan raspberries	Diarrhea, vomit- ing, muscle pain, fatigue	1 week
Giardiasis iardia lamblia)	Contaminated water	Diarrhea, abdominal pain, bloating, heart- burn, anorexia, nausea, vomiting	5-25 days
Trichinosis chinella spiralis)	Raw or undercooked pork and wild game	Fever, abdominal symptoms, joint and muscle pain, headache, facial swelling, painful breathing, muscle weakness	Abdominal symptoms, 1-2 days; further symptoms, 2-8 weeks

COMMON FOODBORNE ILLNESSES

ILLNESS (AND CAUSATIVE ORGANISM)	COMMON FOOD SOURCES	SYMPTOMS	SYMPTOM ON
ILLNESSES CAUSED BY NATURAL TOXINS			
Ciguatera fish poisoning (dinoflagellates)	Warm-water fishes, typically grouper, snapper, amberjack, and barracuda	Numbness and tingling, nausea, vomiting, diarrhea, respiratory paralysis, muscle pain, heart abnormalities	within 6 hou
Scombroid poisoning	Spoiled fish, such as tuna, mackerel, or mahimahi	Nausea, vomiting, headache, thirst, hives, diarrhea, itchiness, tingling of the mouth and throat	Immediate 30 minute
Shellfish poisoning, paralytic	Oysters, clams, mussels, scallops	Paralysis, tingling and numbness, dry throat, incoordination, incoherent speech, respiratory paralysis	30 minutes hours

GLOSSARY

assay An examination to determine the characteristics of something, as well as the presence of one or more components.

calorie In nutrition, a measurement that is used to determine food energy, or the metabolizing value of a food.

carbohydrates Chemical compounds of carbon, hydrogen that provide a primary source of energy; found primarily in sugary and starchy foods.

catabolize A specific type of metabolism involving the release of energy and resulting in the breakdown of complex materials such as proteins.

cellulose A complex carbohydrate, or polysaccharide, consisting of 3,000 or more glucose units.

disaccharide A type of sugar created by combining two monosaccharides (simple sugars) and removing water from the compound's structure.

enzyme A protein that promotes a biochemical reaction, most often causing it to accelerate.

glucose A simple carbohydrate principally used by the human body as fuel for the brain, nervous system, and red blood cells.

insoluble A substance that cannot be dissolved in a liquid.

ketosis The accumulation of organic compounds called ketones in bodily tissue and fluids, the result of the incomplete metabolization of fatty acids.

lactation The process of milk being produced by the mammary glands, or breasts.

lactose The type of sugar found in milk, a disaccharide made up of glucose and galactose.

lipids Substances that, along with proteins and carbohydrates, are essential components of a living organism's cells, such as fats.

metabolism All of the processes by which particular substances (such as nutrients from food) are handled in the living body.

nutrients A substance that sustains and provides energy to a living organism.

pasteurize The act of heating a liquid for a certain amount of time, which kills any harmful microorganisms, such as bacteria.

physiochemical Of or relating to a branch of science that examines physical and chemical properties of substances.

protein An organic compound composed of one or more chains of amino acids and arranged in a complex structure. A protein can contain other components, such as sugar or fat, in addition to amino acids.

provitamin The precursor of a vitamin that can be metabolized into the vitamin by an organism.

satiety The state of being full to or beyond capacity.

sterols A number of different kinds of steroid alcohols (such as cholesterol) distributed throughout animal and plant lipids.

thermic Of or relating to the quality of being thermal, or caused by heat.

triglycerides Any of a group of lipids commonly found in fatty tissue and circulating in the bloodstream of living organisms.

BIBLIOGRAPHY

FOODS

The composition and nutritional value of foods are presented in Jean A. Thompson Pennington and Judith Spungen Douglas, *Bowes and Church's Food Values of Portions Commonly Used*, 19th ed. (2009); and Helen Charley and Connie Weaver, *Foods: A Scientific Approach* (1998). Also useful is Kenneth F. Kiple and Kriemhild Coneè Ornelas (eds.), *The Cambridge World History of Food, 2 vol.* (2000). A challenging view of the economics and politics of food is presented in Marion Nestle, *Food Politics: How the Food Industry Influences Nutrition and Health* (2002).

NUTRITION RECOMMENDATIONS

Recommended nutrient intakes and safe upper limits for various nutrients are detailed in a series of reports by the Institute of Medicine (U.S.): *Dietary Reference Intakes for Calcium, Phosphorus, Magnesium, Vitamin D, and Fluoride* (1997); *Dietary Reference Intakes for Thiamin, Riboflavin, Niacin, Vitamin B6, Folate, Vitamin B12, Pantothenic Acid, Biotin, and Choline* (1998); *Dietary Reference Intakes for Vitamin C, Vitamin E, Selenium, and Carotenoids* (2000); *Dietary Reference Intakes for Vitamin A, Vitamin K, Arsenic, Boron, Chromium, Copper, Iodine, Iron, Manganese, Molybdenum, Nickel, Silicon, Vanadium, and Zinc* (2001); and *Dietary Reference Intakes: Applications in Dietary Assessment* (2001); these reports update and augment the National

Research Council (U.S.), *Recommended Dietary Allowances*, 10th ed. (1989). Dietary guidelines in various countries are presented in "Dietary Guidelines in Three Regions of the World," in Carolyn D. Berdanier (ed.), *Handbook of Nutrition and Food* (2002); United States Department of Agriculture and Department of Health and Human Services, *Nutrition and Your Health: Dietary Guidelines for Americans*, 5th ed. (2000); Health Education Authority, *The Balance of Good Health: Introducing the National Food Guide* (1994); and Health Canada, *Canada's Food Guide to Healthy Eating for People Four Years and Over* (2001).

NUTRITION THROUGHOUT THE LIFE CYCLE

Bonnie S. Worthington-Roberts and Sue Rodwell Williams (eds.), *Nutrition Throughout the Life Cycle*, 4th ed. (2000); William V. Tamborlane (ed.), *The Yale Guide to Children's Nutrition* (1997); and Martha L. Hutchinson and Hamish N. Munro (eds.), *Nutrition and Aging* (1986).

HUMAN METABOLISM, NUTRITION, AND NUTRITIONAL DISEASE

General comprehensive information is presented in James L. Groff and Sareen S. Gropper, *Advanced Nutrition and Human Metabolism*, 3rd ed. (2000); Gordon M. Wardlaw and Carol Byrd-Bredbenner, *Wardlaw's Perspectives in Nutrition*, 9th ed. (2012); L. Kathleen Mahan and Sylvia Escott-Stump (eds.), *Krause's Food & Nutrition Therapy*, 12th ed. (2008); Eleanor Noss Whitney and Sharon Rady Rolfes, *Understanding Nutrition*, 12th ed. (2011); Barbara A. Bowman and Robert M. Russell (eds.), *Present Knowledge in Nutrition,* 9th ed. (2006); Maurice E. Shils (ed.), *Modern Nutrition in Health and Disease*, 10th ed. (2006); Carolyn D.

Berdanier, *Handbook of Nutrition and Food* (2002); Frances Sienkiewicz Sizer and Eleanor Noss Whitney, *Nutrition: Concepts and Controversies,* 9th ed. (2002); Melvin H. Williams, *Nutrition for Health, Fitness, and Sport,* 7th ed. (2004); A. Stewart Truswell, *ABC of Nutrition,* 4th ed. (2003); and Martha H. Stipanuk (ed.), *Biochemical and Physiological Aspects of Human Nutrition* (1999). An overview of trace elements can be found in World Health Organization, *Trace Elements in Human Nutrition and Health* (1996).

WORLD HUNGER AND MALNUTRITION

Useful guides for understanding malnutrition include Thomas J. Marchione (ed.), *Scaling Up; Scaling Down: Overcoming Malnutrition in Developing Countries* (1999); and Frances Moore Lappé and Anna Lappé, *Hope's Edge: The Next Diet for a Small Planet* (2002); Richard D. Semba and Martin W. Bloem (eds.), *Nutrition and Health in Developing Countries* (2001); and Michael C. Latham, *Human Nutrition in the Developing World* (1997).

DIET AND CHRONIC DISEASE

Comprehensive sources on diet and chronic disease are National Research Council (U.S.) Committee on Diet and Health, *Diet and Health: Implications for Reducing Chronic Disease Risk* (1989); and Institute of Medicine (U.S.), *Dietary Reference Intakes*, a series of reports published periodically starting in 1997.

A major international report on diet and cancer prevention is World Cancer Research Fund/American Institute for Cancer Research, *Food, Nutrition, and the Prevention of Cancer: A Global Perspective* (1997). An evaluation of claims for the use of diet, herbs, and supplements in cancer prevention and treatment is American Cancer Society, *Guide to Complementary and Alternative Cancer Methods* (2000).

Practical information for controlling diabetes with proper nutrition is detailed in American Diabetes Association, *Guide to Medical Nutrition Therapy* (1999).

OBESITY AND EATING DISORDERS

The causes and consequences of obesity and a comprehensive framework for treatment are considered in Thomas A. Wadden and Albert J. Stunkard (eds.), *Handbook of Obesity Treatment* (2002). The relationship between body image and eating disorders and approaches to treatment are examined in Ira M. Sacker and Marc A. Zimmer, *Dying to Be Thin: Understanding and Defeating Anorexia Nervosa and Bulimia—A Practical Lifesaving Guide* (1987, rev. ed. 2001); and J. Kevin Thompson and Linda Smolak (eds.), *Body Image, Eating Disorders, and Obesity in Youth: Assessment, Prevention, and Treatment*, 2nd ed. (2009).

FOOD ALLERGIES AND INTOLERANCES

Information about food allergies is presented in Jonathan Brostoff and Linda Gamlin, *Food Allergies and Food Intolerance: The Complete Guide to Their Identification and Treatment* (2000); and Celide Barnes Koerner and Anne Munoz-Furlong, *Food Allergies: How to Eat Safely and Enjoyably* (1998).

INDEX

A

acrylamide toxicity, 192–193
Adequate Intake (AI), 18
alcohol consumption, 86–87, 187
    alcoholism, 126, 130, 133
    effect on health, 142, 144,
        145, 153–154, 158, 161
    limiting, 24, 86, 179
    and pregnancy, 21
Alzheimer's disease, 25–27
anemia, 101–102, 131, 133–134
arthritis, 25
attention-deficit/hyperactivity
    disorder (ADHD), 23

B

basal metabolic rate (BMR), 7–8
beriberi, 17, 53, 78, 126, 127–128
bioflavonoids, 69
blood lipoproteins, and
    role of diet, 149–159
body fat, 9–11
body mass, 9
body mass index (BMI),
    10, 170–171
bovine spongiform
    encephalopathy, 198–199
bowel conditions and
    diseases, 180–181
Boyd Orr, John, 98–99

C

caffeine, 21, 86, 179, 187
calcium, 44, 45, 50, 110–111
    deficiency, 101, 106–107, 120
calories, and energy, 4–5
cancer, 1, 17, 192, 193
    breast, 161–162
    colorectal, 107, 160
    and obesity, 157, 160, 161, 170
    prostate, 160–161
    role of diet in, 141–142, 156–162
carbohydrates, 28–34, 49
    deficiency, 99–100
    dietary fibre, 32–34
    glucose, 29, 32
    other sugars and starch, 30–32
cardiovascular/heart disease,
    1, 17, 23, 24
    role of diet in, 37, 141–156
carnitine, 69
celiac disease, 186–187
chemicals and food safety, 191–195
chloride, 44, 45, 46, 108
chlorine deficiency, 108–109
cholesterol, 37–38, 51, 143,
    149–150, 151, 152, 153
choline, 43, 67–68
constipation, 180
copper, 44, 46, 113
cultural differences in nutrition,
    11–12, 13